T0244536

FATE DEALS
A HAND

FATE DEALS
A HAND

THE SLIPPERY FORTUNES OF
TITANIC'S PROFESSIONAL GAMBLERS

GEORGE BEHE

Front cover images, top: RMS *Titanic* departs Southampton on her maiden
voyage (author's collection). *Bottom:* White Star Line playing card and chip
(author's collection); other playing cards (spxChrome/iStock).
Back cover image: Text based on a White Star Line notice. (Author's collection)

First published 2023

The History Press
97 St George's Place, Cheltenham,
Gloucestershire, GL50 3QB
www.thehistorypress.co.uk

British Library Cataloguing in Publication Data.
A catalogue record for this book is available from the British Library.

ISBN 978 1 80399 238 9

Typesetting and origination by The History Press
Printed and bound in Great Britain by TJ Books Limited, Padstow, Cornwall.

Trees for LYfe

BY THE SAME AUTHOR

Titanic: Psychic Forewarnings of a Tragedy
(Patrick Stephens, 1988)

Lost at Sea: Ghost Ships and Other Mysteries, with Michael Goss
(Prometheus Books, 1994)

Titanic: Safety, Speed and Sacrifice
(Transportation Trails, 1997)

'Archie': The Life of Major Archibald Butt from Georgia to the Titanic
(Lulu.com Press, 2010)

A Death on the Titanic: The Loss of Major Archibald Butt
(Lulu.com Press, 2011)

On Board RMS Titanic: Memories of the Maiden Voyage
(The History Press, 2012)

Voices from the Carpathia: Rescuing RMS Titanic
(The History Press, 2015)

Titanic Memoirs
(three volumes, Lulu.com Press, 2015)

The Titanic Files: A Paranormal Sourcebook
(Lulu.com Press, 2015)

Titanic: The Return Voyage
(Lulu.com Press, 2020)

'Those Brave Fellows': The Last Hours of the Titanic's Band
(Lulu.com Press, 2020)

The Titanic: Disaster: A Medical Dossier
(Lulu.com Press, 2021)

Letters from Titanic: Fine Press Edition
(The History Press, 2022)

CONTENTS

ACKNOWLEDGEMENTS

Several people were of great help to me while I was doing research for this book. Don Lynch, Philip Gowan, Mike Herbold, Hermann Söldner, Patrick Fitch and Brandon Whited all contributed important pieces to the puzzle, and I am deeply grateful to each of them for their assistance. Sandy Cottrell, reference librarian at the Macomb County Library, went to great lengths to obtain obscure 1912 newspaper microfilms for me, without which this book could not have been written. A special word of thanks goes to Bonnie Berg, who created the book's pen-and-ink illustrations depicting the *Titanic*'s gamblers.

Finally, I owe a great debt of gratitude to someone I'll never be able to repay. In September 1981 I first contacted Wallace B. Yates of Findlay, Ohio. Wally had carried memories of his conversation with Hanna Yates for half a century and very kindly answered the many questions I put to him. Wally and his wife Mabel travelled many miles in an effort to obtain new information about Jay Yates but were unable to find anything more. Wally's own personal recollections were apparently the only ones extant in the Yates family, and it was with great sadness that, just two months after contacting him, I learned of his death on 2 December 1981, shortly after he suffered a heart attack. I hope my use of the information Wally gave me will, in some measure, repay the tremendous debt of gratitude I owe him. Mr Yates showed great interest in my project, and I hope he would have been pleased with the end result.

INTRODUCTION

It is a well-known fact that professional gamblers and con men secretly patronised the card rooms of transatlantic passenger liners during the nineteenth and early twentieth centuries, and that these men often concluded their voyages in possession of more money than they started out with. The present author first revealed the existence of *Titanic*'s professional gamblers in 1982, when his article on the subject was published in the autumn and winter 1982 issues of *The Commutator*, the official journal of the Titanic Historical Society.

Unfortunately, in those pre-internet days serious researchers were forced either to borrow newspaper microfilms via interlibrary loan or else make personal visits to distant archives that did not participate in the interlibrary loan programme. The financial expense of making far-flung research trips severely limited the historical resources researchers were able to access in those days, and these informational gaps caused unavoidable historical errors to creep into *Titanic* books and articles that were being written during that period.

Times have changed, and nowadays electronic access to many archival collections has made it possible for researchers to rapidly sift through distant historical sources and uncover new information that otherwise might never have seen the light of day. This happened in the case for my ongoing research into the lives of *Titanic*'s professional gamblers, and I have taken full advantage of this present opportunity to correct a couple of historical mistakes in my original essay and add a great deal of new information that has come to light during the decades that have elapsed since its original publication.

This book is the author's best attempt to present the definitive story of the three professional gamblers who survived the sinking of the *Titanic*.

George Behe
Grand Rapids, Michigan, 2023

LUODOVIC RADZEVIL AND 'BUD' HAUSER

The year was 1913, and Austrian barber Luodovic Radzevil found himself in dire straits when it became necessary for him to flee to England to avoid being conscripted into the army. After crossing the English Channel almost penniless, Radzevil began to evolve a plan whereby he could stave off starvation and perhaps even turn a tidy profit. The ex-barber must have had prior experience as a confidence man, because his scheme required such boldness and nerve that only an experienced practitioner of the art could have pulled it off.

Radzevil had learned his awkward, archaic English by studying a Bible. (Although its moral precepts were apparently lost on him, the Good Book at least made it possible for Radzevil to make himself understood.) Armed with this limited fluency in the language, Radzevil appeared at the White Star Line offices and offered his services as a steerage interpreter, claiming that he knew all the necessary European, Asian and African tongues.

The White Star official conducting the interview must have smiled sceptically as he asked the Austrian to say something in Chinese, but without hesitation the undaunted Radzevil asked the official to pose a question in Chinese so that he could answer it in the same language. Incredibly, on the strength of this audacious bluff, Radzevil got the job as interpreter for the White Star Line. His terms for employment were very simple: he wanted the equivalent of $10 in advance, a first-class passage to America and a blue uniform adorned with gold braid – and he received all three.

Using his cash advance, Radzevil instructed a printer to produce calling cards bearing his name and the title 'official interpreter'. He then repaired to a holding area where emigrants were awaiting passage on a White Star ship and handed out his cards to these future steerage passengers. Although many people could not read the cards, they were suitably impressed and cowed by Radzevil's resplendent blue uniform.

Next, the con man hurried to a nearby barber shop, where he determined the price of a haircut to be sixpence. Radzevil told the proprietor that a great crowd of customers would be arriving within the next fifteen minutes and would be presenting his 'official interpreter' cards. Radzevil instructed the barber to raise his prices for these people, charging two shillings per haircut and one shilling for a shave, and he specified that he would return later to collect 50 per cent of the barber's inflated profits.

Rushing back to the holding area, Radzevil acquired a megaphone and informed the emigrants that the White Star Line required them to get a haircut and shave before boarding the ship, and for the next three days the barber shop was inundated with steerage passengers dutifully obeying the interpreter's instructions. By the time it was over, Radzevil and the barber had both reaped a handsome financial reward from the transaction.

Next, the Austrian instructed the emigrants to visit a certain hardware store and purchase hunting knives as protection from the Native Americans who were rampaging in America, and the unfortunate people meekly followed his instructions. The interpreter was making plans for them to purchase new suits of clothing and visit a Turkish bath, but the White Star Line interrupted things by ordering the steerage passengers aboard ship.

Radzevil had planned ahead for this eventuality and is said to have had his cabin stocked with barrels of apples. The fruit was sold to his charges at two shillings each to supplement their diet of steerage food.

When the ship finally reached New York, Radzevil debarked with new luggage, a new wardrobe, hundreds of dollars and the names and addresses of 1,500 immigrants – but he was not finished with them yet. The interpreter rushed out and rented an office in Manhattan before hurrying back to where the immigrants were awaiting clearance through customs. Addressing the crowd, Radzevil informed everyone that he would continue to work for their well-being in the United States and that if anyone wished to send money back to the Old Country, he would be happy to arrange the transaction. Radzevil also promised to arrange a military service exemption for anyone who wanted it (even though America had no draft at the time).

As the months went by, many of the immigrants came to Radzevil's office to take advantage of his generous offer of help and entrusted money to him for transmission to relatives in Europe. When they later enquired why the money did not reach its intended destination, the wily Austrian blamed the mail service and implied that greedy mail clerks were stealing the funds. To allay suspicion, Radzevil carefully kept track of his customers' losses and promised that his friend the president would assist him in the coming investigation.

This lucrative arrangement continued for several years until, by chance, the Austrian Consul got wind of the situation and informed the postal authorities, who quickly brought Radzevil's career to a close.

The story of Luodovic Radzevil's lengthy confidence game was first presented in a book by Jay Nash titled *Hustlers and Con Men*, but this kind of prolonged bilking of victims was not a usual feature of the typical shipboard bunco game. Most con men who operated on the great passenger liners brought their game to an end at the termination of a voyage, thus facilitating a quick, clean getaway with their ill-gotten gains. In addition, these grifters rarely attempted to cheat passengers in steerage and instead preferred to target rich passengers in first class, a practice that usually netted the con man a much higher profit margin in return for his time and effort.

The simplest way for a bunco artist to achieve his goal was to engage a potential victim in a dishonest game of cards. The smoking rooms and private cabins of the ocean greyhounds were usually the settings for these card games, and those belonging to the White Star Line were no exception. In our examination of these professional gamblers, let us leave Luodovic Radzevil and go back one year to 1912 – a year that several sharps would always remember and a year that brought the career (and life) of at least one other seagoing professional gambler to an abrupt close.

When B.J. 'Bud' Hauser boarded the *Olympic* at Southampton on 3 April 1912 he undoubtedly intended to arrive in New York with more money than he set out with. (He had done it many times before, the *Olympic* herself having been the setting for six prior coups.) Hauser was a man accustomed to living by his wits, and – had fate not intervened – this voyage might have proved just as profitable as the others. You see, Bud Hauser was a 'sporting man', a euphemism used early in the twentieth century to denote a professional gambler and confidence man.

Like many a sharper, Hauser made his living on board the ocean greyhounds and, by spending his evenings at cards in the smoking rooms, he could usually relieve unwary passengers of any superfluous cash they might be carrying. He was good at it, too, because his fine appearance and hearty manner served to disarm anyone who might suspect him of less-than-honourable intentions.

But Hauser's wholesome demeanour was just the masquerade of a first-rate card mechanic. It was he who originated a novel method of cheating at bridge when the game was still new. (Hauser engaged a New York millionaire in a 'friendly' game but stationed a confederate in such a position that the millionaire's hand was visible to him;

B.J. 'Bud' Hauser.

the confederate, by the way he smoked his cigarettes and the drinks he ordered, conveyed information to Hauser about the victim's cards, and the millionaire walked away from the table $60,000 poorer but perhaps a little wiser.)

Of course, Bud Hauser did not become a consummate con artist overnight. He was born in New York around 1874 and was one of three brothers who were taken west when they were very young. In 1894 Hauser returned to New York as the possessor of very definite sporting tendencies and brought with him a string of horses. Aided by a stable badge, he posed as an authorised betting commissioner – a ruse that continued until the Pinkerton Agency told him he was barred from all metropolitan racetracks.

After this setback, Hauser concentrated on improving his digital dexterity and developed a reputation as an excellent card mechanic and con man. After he began to travel outside New York he was arrested in Chicago for swindling a man out of $4,000. In 1900 he was back in New York and formed a temporary partnership with his brother George, and together they lured a man off an ocean liner and took him to Kid McCoy's saloon. There they administered knockout drops to the unsuspecting pigeon and robbed him of bonds valued at $3,000. Hauser was eventually picked up by the authorities but was discharged when it was learned that the victim had returned to Europe.

At various points during his nefarious career Hauser was arrested on both sides of the Atlantic. In 1902 he was accused of a robbery in New York but was released on $3,000 bond. He promptly dropped out of sight and, for the next six years, he succeeded in eluding the district attorney. In 1908 he finally slipped up by assaulting a man in the café of the Waldorf-Astoria, which led to his capture on the old charge of jumping bond.

In December 1908 Hauser was arrested once again on Broadway after advertising in the newspapers (using the alias McCafferty) that he would give tips on the horse races and pick a winner every day.

At about this time he began to travel the ocean liners utilising his expertise in card and dice manipulation. On 31 December 1910, upon the arrival of the Cunard liner *Campania*, Hauser was arrested as a dice swindler.

Despite his many arrests, Hauser actually spent very little time behind bars. In fact, his friends all claimed he was never convicted of any crime, even though he was often apprehended and accused. Hauser had good looks and a hearty, breezy manner that seemed to make his victims reluctant to appear against him in court, and so the gambler's sea-going career flourished. He often teamed with other 'deep-water men' like W.J. 'Doc' Owen, Colonel Torrey (Willie Green), George McMullen and Frankie Dwyer, and these confidence men would divide up the spoils of war at the conclusion of each voyage.

Hauser usually booked onto a ship using the pseudonym 'Barton J. Harvey', letting it be understood that he was a son of the Harvey who founded the system of hotels and cafes on the Atchison, Topeka and Santa Fe railroad system. Byron J. Harvey, the true son of the restaurateur, was well aware of Hauser's use of the family name; indeed, 'Barton J. Harvey' was often mistaken for Byron Harvey due to the similarity in names, and the gambler did nothing to discourage this confusion.

Hauser was using the Harvey alias on his 3 April 1912 trip on board the *Olympic*, and the voyage to New York was proceeding smoothly. He was described as the liveliest man in the smoking room and caused much comment by the 'reckless' way he played cards and the great diversity of his alcoholic refreshment (absinthe, straight rye whiskey, champagne, and more). He also made a daily visit to the ship's Turkish bath, perhaps attempting to blunt the after-effects of his nightly revelry. Every evening at around 9 p.m., however, our man would abandon the social atmosphere of the smoking room and retire to the privacy of his stateroom. It was rumoured that he and several other passengers played cards there until the wee hours, but no detailed information is known. It was later claimed that on the first day of the voyage Hauser and his fellow grifters fleeced *Olympic*'s passengers of a sum approaching $10,000.

On the evening of 9 April 1912 Hauser, as usual, had been drinking rather immoderately, and as 9 p.m. approached he lay down his cards and left the smoking room. After stopping off to enjoy another brief session in the Turkish bath, he retired to his stateroom. What happened to him after that is uncertain, and it is possible the facts were deliberately obscured by the gambler's colleagues.

In the stateroom next to Hauser was a man who booked on the passenger list as 'A. McClellan'. At about 5 a.m. the next morning, when *Olympic* was 150 miles east of Ambrose Channel, 'McClellan' said he heard a commotion in Hauser's stateroom followed by the sound of a man groaning. He arose and went next door, where he found the gambler tossing around on his bed with a cold breeze sweeping through the room. 'McClellan' called a steward, who immediately notified ship's doctor J.C.H. Beaumont. Upon entering Hauser's stateroom, Dr Beaumont found his patient lying in his berth dressed only in his underclothing, semi-conscious and groaning from the severe pain in his heart region. Stimulants were administered to the stricken man, but they had no effect. The physician remained with Hauser until 7.55 a.m., at which time the gambler expired. It was said that three other professional gamblers who were on board *Olympic* were acting as nurses in the stateroom when Hauser died.

When word of Bud Hauser's death leaked out, rumours raced through the *Olympic*'s company like wildfire. One of the most common stories was that 'Barton Harvey' had lost heavily at cards to a group of professional gamblers (!) and had died of a heart attack in his stateroom. Another story claimed that 'Harvey' had won a large amount of money from several gamblers and was so slow to pay the debts he had incurred earlier that the gamblers attacked him in the smoking room, after which he retired to his stateroom and died of his injuries.

When the *Olympic* docked in New York on the afternoon of 10 April 1912, the ship's officers denied these rumours. Dr Beaumont reported that 'Harvey' had died of 'heart disease following alcoholic poisoning'. The physician even sent a telegram to the Harvey family notifying them of their 'son's' passing, and detectives employed by the White Star Line went aboard the *Olympic* to investigate the death.

A reporter on the dock managed to interview 'A. McClellan', the man who had discovered Hauser's plight. 'McClellan', a soft-spoken Australian, well groomed with a neat black moustache, told the reporter that 'Barton Harvey' must have fallen asleep without covering himself and that the combination of a cold draft, recent Turkish bath and alcohol would have been enough to kill any man. The reporter queried the Australian about the rumours of large gambling stakes during the voyage, and 'McClellan' laughed and said he had won more money on a single horse race or a single hand of cards than had changed hands during the *Olympic's* entire voyage. He told the reporter, 'A five-pound note was the biggest bet I saw made, and that was on the ship's pool.'

The reporter happened to notice a curious fact while he was interviewing 'A. McClellan'. The man's baggage was sitting on the dock next to him, but the name printed on it was 'A. McLenna'. The reporter did not know he had been questioning George McMullen (also known as 'Australian Pete' and 'The Indiana Wonder') and that McMullen was a card sharp and one of Bud Hauser's regular travelling companions. For that reason alone, it is almost certain that McMullen did not tell the reporter everything he knew about Hauser's final hours. (As will be seen, professional sharps could be both inventive and reticent when asked to tell the truth about their activities.)

Four or five additional sharps were on board the *Olympic* during this crossing, and before the ship docked one of them sent a wireless to New York informing fellow con artists of Hauser's passing. A delegation of sharpers went down to the dock to meet the *Olympic* and bid farewell to their departed brother-in-arms. These men met with the sharps who made the crossing and discussed the many stories told about Hauser. It was learned that gambling profits had indeed been very small on this crossing, the potential victims having been very conservative at betting. As was common among bunco men, the sharpers showed little sympathy or concern for their late associate, and the last we hear of Bud Hauser is that his body was 'awaiting any undertaker who may call for it'.

The death of a well-known professional gambler on board the *Olympic* was no doubt a great embarrassment to the White Star Line, but this awkward state of affairs was completely forgotten in light of events that were to occur only four days later. For on 10 April, the same morning that Bud Hauser died, the *Olympic*'s younger sister was beginning the first day of her maiden voyage – and she, like the *Olympic*, was carrying a full complement of sporting men.

THE GAMBLING TECHNIQUES

The advent of regular passenger services across the North Atlantic was a godsend to both European and American confidence men. After booking passage on one of the ocean greyhounds, a professional gambler could leisurely browse through the first-class passenger list in search of suitable quarry. After finding a potential victim, the gambler might engage his target in casual conversation, always taking care to ask about the man's family. This was not only disarming, but it also helped the gambler to judge his victim's standard of living and approximate worth. A crossing of five or six days would give the sharp ample time to cultivate the good will of his intended victim, which was usually not too difficult. People always seemed to be less suspicious of strangers on board a ship than anywhere else, and it was this trusting, naïve attitude that brought more than one ocean traveller to the brink of financial ruin.

It did not take long for the shipping lines to realise that professional gamblers were present on their ships. Many lines tried to make their passengers aware of the problem by printing cautionary statements in their passenger lists as well as on signs posted in the smoking rooms. Many passengers enjoyed their card games too much to be deterred by these warnings, though, and many of these people eventually fell into the waiting hands of a sharper.

'It has always puzzled me why passengers, who are usually men of a certain amount of common sense, allow themselves to be fleeced by the professional gamblers who frequently cross in the large passenger steamers,' Captain Bertram Hayes once wrote in regard to the gamblers who booked passage on his own White Star vessels. He continued:

Most of these gentlemen carry the trademarks of their profession written all over their faces, and one would think that alone would prevent others from associating with them in any way, let alone from playing games of chance with them. There are exceptions, and I remember one man being pointed out to me who had the manners of the proverbial meek and mild curate, and dressed himself in a kind of a clerical costume to assist him in his business. For the first few days he played with the children on deck and so ingratiated himself with the parents, and I heard that he made a very good haul during the last day or so of the passage ... Most of them are well-known to the office staff, and also to the ship's people, and I should think it must be a little disconcerting to them to be greeted by the Second Steward when making application for their seats at table with the remark, 'What name this time, sir?' as very often happens. The police on either side of the Atlantic, too, inform us when they know that any of them are crossing.

Hayes went on to explain:

We cannot refuse to carry them, as steamship companies are what is known as 'common carriers', and by law are compelled to sell a ticket to anyone who has the money to pay for it and whose papers are in order, providing there is accommodation available in the ship … Short of actually pointing them out to each individual, every effort is made on the ship to protect their fellow passengers from them. Notices are printed in the passenger lists which everyone gets, and, in addition, notices are posted in the public rooms warning people not to play cards with people whom they don't know, as professional gamblers are known to be on board. Yet they somehow manage to ingratiate themselves, and I have had many complaints from passengers who have been fleeced. They seldom, if ever, play for high stakes in the smoke room; that is usually done in their own staterooms or in those of their victims.

Travelling first class on a great ocean liner was a mark of prestige for 'people of quality', and it was natural to assume that one's fellow passengers were of the same respectable social standing as oneself. These people often welcomed the opportunity to spend much of the voyage engaged in a game of poker or bridge whist. It was a chance to relax with old friends and new acquaintances, enjoy good fellowship and conversation, and to test one's skill at his favourite game of cards. Under circumstances like these, the thought of one player deliberately cheating the others rarely occurred to the average player until it was too late, but there was always a ready supply of card mechanics ready and willing to apply the shears to the sheep.

These men were aware that, in cards, manipulation was more profit-able than speculation.

There were two varieties of these boatmen – the amateur cheat and the true professional. The amateur was a man who had a legitimate means of earning a living and only cheated at cards to supplement his income. His basic reason for cheating was greed, but sometimes a man might have a psychological need to win at any cost. One might think these part-time cheats were apt to be small-time businessmen, but this was not always so. Many of those who were ultimately exposed as cheats proved to be very wealthy people, sometimes even millionaires. One of these men, when caught, explained that he was financially secure on paper, but that certain business setbacks often caused him great difficulty in securing ready cash to meet his pay-rolls. Cheating at cards provided him with that ready cash.

In a different league altogether was the professional gambler. Whereas the amateur cheat was motivated by greed, it has been said that the professional was actuated by love of the game itself. Winning was not his sole delight, but equal pleasure was derived from 'making the hazard'. A man who made a successful living from card manipulation lived under the constant threat of exposure, and this fact made him prone to thrive on the danger involved. As one gambler put it, 'I cannot understand honest men. They live desper-ate lives, full of boredom.' The professional enjoyed matching his wits and skill against the untrained senses of his intended victims, and he usually succeeded in his efforts. His winnings were called 'pretty money' and were generally spent very freely, the gambler being both generous and careless with his bankroll. On those rare occasions when fate went against his best efforts, the professional sharp was normally philosophical about his losses. Strangely enough, it was usually the amateur cheat who was the hardest loser, since the professional took both prosperity and adversity in his stride and recognised that an occasional loss was inevitable.

Captain Bertram Hayes once wrote:

Personally, I have no sympathy with anyone who loses money to them, and when they come to me for advice as to the best means of getting it back, I always say the same thing: 'If you had taken my advice, or rather the company's, you would not have lost your money. The only thing to do, if you consider you have been swindled and have paid by check, is to stop the check by wireless and stand the consequences.' Sometimes out of curiosity I ask them: 'Would you have taken his money providing you had been allowed to win?' And they always answer: 'Yes.' They acknowledge, too, that they have read the notices warning them against playing with strangers, and sometimes add in mitigation of their foolishness: 'But I had a few drinks before the smoke room closed, and they followed me down to my room, and it was there I lost my money.'

'Doc' Owen.

Captain Hayes recalled how a well-known professional once attempted to gain the good will and trust of his fellow passengers on board a certain White Star vessel under Hayes's command:

> The proudest man that I think I have ever carried was a well-known gambler, 'Doc' Owen by name … It was some years ago that he embarked at Liverpool on the old *Majestic* carrying a large silver loving cup under his arm, which he said had been presented to him by his fellow passengers on the *Celtic*, by which ship he had crossed to England, as a token of their regard for him. The inscription on the cup bore out his statement, and he never seemed to tire of showing it to everybody while he was with us, crew as well as passengers.

John Neville Maskelyne, the noted nineteenth-century stage conjuror and card expert, wrote that the American card sharper was better able to make a successful living than his English counterpart. Many of the older methods of cheating were tolerably well known to American gamblers but were practically unknown in England. According to Maskelyne, the average English sharp was 'in a condition of unsophisticated innocence' compared to a professional gambler from the United States. Yankee ingenuity apparently came to the fore whenever newer and better methods of card manipulation were found to be necessary.

But whatever the nationality of an ocean gambler might be, they all shared certain personality traits that were absolutely necessary if they were to make a successful living in their chosen field. Boldness and nerve were essential. The boatman needed to have supreme confidence in his own ability to invisibly manipulate the cards under the very noses of his intended victims. He needed tact and address, because his deportment would determine the level of society in which he would be enabled to work his wiles. A certain amount of initial reserve and dignity was desirable in the opening stages of targeting a wealthy victim, but after the first acquaintance was made the sharp would affect a friendly camaraderie that would completely disarm the unsuspecting dupe. This friendliness was simply a part of the act, because a conscience was not usually in the sharp's make-up. A few of the more 'genteel' con men would operate according to the philosophy 'never send them to the river', meaning they would never bilk a victim to the point where he would commit suicide, but the more typical grifter did not worry about the possible consequences of his shady dealings. This type of gambler was generally pretty cold-blooded and would not hesitate to 'gull the mark' for as much money as he possibly could.

There was one more requirement that was absolutely essential to a professional card mechanic: skill coupled with uniformity of action. It was pointless for a sharper to secretly manipulate the cards if, in doing so, he called attention to it by departing from his customary method of holding or handling the deck. The card mechanic learned to handle the deck the same way whether he was playing fairly or not.

In order to simplify this handling of the deck, most boatmen specialised in a single card game, some preferring poker while others chose bridge whist. With only one game to worry about, a sharper could usually perfect two or three sleights with the cards that were especially useful in his chosen game. Indeed, by using these few secret moves sparingly during a game, the sharp would usually wind up a winner. One boatman told a friend he had spent ten years perfecting a move called 'culling the deck' (accumulating a known good hand on the bottom of the deck while shuffling). Using just this one sleight enabled the gambler to earn a very good living.

Contrary to the popular impression, a lone sharper did not play dishonestly during an entire card game. To do so would have been professional suicide, since no player normally won repeatedly during any given game. The professional card mechanic played fairly whenever possible, since this minimised the chances of his being exposed.

Besides, manipulation was not always necessary for him to win. 'Show me a drinking card player, and I'll show you one I can take – honestly,' one veteran boatman related fondly. Liquor, particularly whisky, clouded the victim's judgement and memory and encouraged recklessly heavy betting. Knowing this, a transatlantic gambler was not about to take unnecessary risks. He would usually feign indifferent play in order to conceal his skill, because two or three crucial wins during the course of the evening would usually suffice for the sharp to make an acceptable margin of profit for the voyage. A spotlessly clean reputation was a card mechanic's sole hope for continued success, because with it he could make a good living from regular customers who would not hesitate to engage him in repeated games of cards.

If even a hint of suspicion attached itself to a professional gambler it usually meant he must resign himself to a wasted voyage, because word would inevitably spread among the passengers that he was thought to have cheated at cards. This tainted reputation could have far-reaching effects on the gambler's life, because if any of the present passengers should share a future voyage with him they would promptly warn their friends of his presence on board.

A passenger who suspected that he had been fleeced by a professional gambler often had to be satisfied with just that – suspicion. A typical card player had little knowledge of the many techniques used by a grifter, since the boatman could execute many sleights right under his victim's nose without the mark being any the wiser. It did not pay for a victim to come right out and accuse a boatman of cheating, because even if the mark thought he had detected a false move on the part of the mechanic, he had no proof that anything illegal had taken place. To complicate things, a ship in international waters was not able to invoke any national statutes concerning crooked gambling. The wisest thing for a victim to do was to report his suspicion to the purser, who would then post the 'professional gamblers aboard' notice in the card rooms. There were several steps that could be taken next.

Occasionally, justice could be served using mere bluff. Through sheer repetition, Captain Arthur Rostron became familiar with victims of the 'Mississippi Heart Hand' (a special bridge hand that was dealt to a victim and looked unbeatable but was not). Confronting the accused cheats with his limited knowledge of their techniques and threatening to have them arrested, Rostron was sometimes able to secure refunds for the victims. This was not to be counted upon regularly, though.

A second possibility was to have the suspected gambler secretly watched during a game. A boatman would sometimes resort to using secret devices to assist him in cheating, and with great good luck he could be caught red-handed while using one of these devices – the only proof needed to establish his guilt.

A more productive procedure was for the captain to send enquiries by wireless concerning the gambler's passport, since many sharps preferred to impersonate wealthy businessmen whose faces were not as well known as their names. Other grifters used names that were phonetically similar to their own names. In either case, their passports were taken out under these assumed names; this was a federal offence when proved, so if a gambler was unlucky enough to receive this unwanted attention he could find himself in very serious trouble.

One final possibility was to set a trap for the suspected crooked gamblers on shore and obtain evidence of a crime committed within some specific national jurisdiction. One victim, after losing $51,000 in a crooked shipboard bridge game, arranged for Michael MacDougall (a gambling expert) to impersonate a wealthy sucker in New York City. A bridge game was arranged in a hotel room with the gamblers who had fleeced the original victim, but, unknown to the grifters, the adjoining room contained three detectives. Needless to say, a conviction was forthcoming.

A discussion of ocean gamblers would not be complete without a brief review of some of the methods they used to fleece a chosen lamb. The boldness and nerve of these men will quickly become apparent, and the reader may also gain an appreciation of their finesse and polished technique.

John Neville Maskelyne's book describing dishonest gambling techniques, *Sharps and Flats*, contains a brief description of the hierarchy of dishonest card techniques given by a professional sharp. This man was training a young friend in the art of cheating and described the three classes of gambler, ranking them in ascending order of success.

1. The first and riskiest branch of the profession was that in which the gambler secretly manipulated the deck in order to achieve his ends. According to Maskelyne's sharper, these men always got caught in the long run.

As has been mentioned, some of these men resorted to secret apparatus to assist them in their efforts. A device called a 'holdout' could be strapped to the chest inside the sharper's shirt, and a Jacob's ladder extended partially down his sleeve that, when desired, would extend down as far as the sharp's wrist. This was used to either secretly deliver good cards to his hand or hold back certain cards for future use.

Other grifters used a device called a 'shiner', which was nothing more than a highly polished object placed on the card table in front of the gambler. While dealing, the sharp could observe the reflection of the cards in the shiner and obtain a distinct edge over his opponent. A shiner could be as simple as an ashtray, finger ring or cufflink, but some were more specialised. One was specially made to fit inside the bowl of a pipe that could then be 'casually' placed in front of the gambler.

These devices could be useful to a sharp but, of course, would sound his death knell if he was ever observed using them, because a gambler would be hard put to deny his guilt in using a holdout that was of no discernible use to an honest player. Consequently, many sharps preferred to make their living by relying solely on their own manual dexterity with a pack of cards.

Many of the sleights used by a sharper were extremely subtle, and 'culling the deck' has already been mentioned. In gathering up cards after a play, the sharp could also 'stock' the deck, gathering known cards into one group. A sharp with good recall could 'count down' and memorise the order of fifteen or twenty cards as they were gathered prior to the shuffle, and just to ensure that this order was not disturbed, he would utilise a 'false shuffle'. This was, to all appearances, a normal shuffle, the only difference being that the order of the memorised cards was not disturbed. The sharp could then offer the deck to his opponent for a cut but, in picking up the deck again, the sharp would 'negate the cut' by using one of many moves to restore the deck to its former order.

2. The second (and better) class of gambler was the group that used marked cards. These 'paper workers' would make extremely subtle markings with India ink on the backs of their cards, each mark indicating the card's value. If a sharp was able to introduce these prepared cards into a game, victory was almost assured.

The great advantage of using marked cards was that they could be played 'honestly' or 'dishonestly' according to the whim of the grifter. In playing them 'honestly', the sharp would merely read the values of his opponent's cards as they were dealt and would then play his own hand against the known hand of the victim. If the victim's hand was the better of the two, the gambler could merely drop out and minimise his losses. With no sleight-of-hand to be detected, the sharp ran a minimal risk of discovery – even by another sharp.

Marked cards played 'honestly' once resulted in a rather humorous confrontation between two sporting men as they sat in on a game. Neither knew that the other was a card mechanic, and the players continued their game in ignorance of that fact for a short time. After a while, though, one of the sharps began to win fairly consistently and his opponent began to get suspicious. His trained eye told him that no sleight-of-hand was being used, so he finally decided that the cards must be marked, even though he could not tell how. In gathering the discarded hands into the deck, he decided to memorise the top eight or ten cards and then threw the deck down on the table, declaring grimly that someone had marked the cards. To prove his point, he began to name the top few cards before he turned them face up. The game ended with all the players staring suspiciously at each other, wondering who the guilty party was. Later, after the players had scattered, the accuser was quietly approached by the first sharp who admitted the cards were his and asked the second sharp what his losses were. Upon being told, the first cheat reimbursed his accuser and then asked his accuser a question that had been baffling him ever since the game ended; the first gambler had only marked the cards for numerical value and was dying to know how the second sharp had been able to name the different suits as well!

Marked cards could also be played 'dishonestly' during the sharp's deal. If he saw that he was about to deal the victim a good card, the sharp could execute a 'bottom deal' or else 'deal seconds'. Using the bottom deal, the sharp could hold back the good card for himself and deal the victim a poor card from the bottom of the deck. When dealing seconds, his thumb would pull the desirable top card slightly aside and the next card down would be dealt to the victim instead.

Learning to bottom deal undetectably was very difficult, since the hand holding the deck would often make a characteristic movement as the crooked deal was being executed. In order to eliminate this telltale movement, some sharps had the last joint of their index finger amputated so that it would not get in the way of a flawless bottom deal, and for many years, to engage in a card game with a man having this small deformity was an unwise move. One such man was closely observed in a shipboard game by Michael MacDougall, but the elderly gentleman appeared to be playing fairly. Instead, a young woman across the table was detected using a bottom deal; it turned out she was the old man's daughter and he had had the foresight to teach her his craft against the day when his hands eventually lost their sureness.

Another risk in bottom dealing was that the cards might 'talk'. Unless great care was used, a card dealt from the bottom of the deck would make a telltale noise that was distinctly different from that of a fairly dealt card. A trained person could simply listen to the cards being dealt and tell when the crooked deal took place.

An amateur cheat was once 'auditioning' before John Phillip Quinn (a professional sharp) in the hope of being accepted into the 'gang'. He proudly showed Quinn his bottom deal, and the professional told the amateur he would be hired only on the following set of conditions:

(1) The amateur must always work with a partner.
(2) The amateur must signal his partner before dealing a card from the bottom of the deck.
(3) The partner would then fire a revolver into the air to cover the terrible noise made when the amateur executed his bottom deal.

A marked deck of cards was once instrumental in breaking off the engagement of two young passengers on an ocean liner. The young man was travelling with his fiancée and her family, but passed much of his time sitting in a cabin playing cards with several other passengers. After only one day of this, the captain received an anonymous note saying that the young man was winning heavily and was suspected of cheating. Upon investigation by Michael MacDougall, the cards were determined to be marked, so the captain confined the youth to his cabin despite the lad's protestations of innocence. For the next several days, however, the same card game continued in the same cabin, and curiosity prompted MacDougall to secretly observe the game. Pretty soon he saw one of the players dealing seconds, and a wireless enquiry to New York revealed that his passenger list name was false. It turned out that the sharp had been hired by a jilted suitor of the girl in question; the sharp was instructed to use marked cards to deal winning hands to the young man and allow him to win often enough to arouse suspicion. The sharp had then sent the anonymous note to the captain. Upon learning of this scheme, the captain immediately released the young man from his cabin and sent along his profuse apologies, but the mere stigma of the accusation caused the girl to break off her engagement, thus achieving the goal of the jilted suitor. The plot would have gone undiscovered had the sharp not succumbed to the temptation of manipulating his marked cards to fleece an extra couple of lambs.

Even if a sharp was unable to introduce his own marked cards into play, he could still mark enough cards in an honest deck to serve his purpose. Enter the 'shade man', 'sand man' and 'punch man'.

The shade man utilised a thin dye the same colour as the deck of cards; the dye container was clipped out of sight under his coat, and when the sharp wished to mark a card he would get a little dye on his thumb and lightly smear it on the card's back. This dye was so thin that the dab of colour was almost invisible to the uninitiated honest player.

The sand man utilised a tiny piece of sandpaper to secretly roughen the edges of the cards according to his own marking system. The sandpaper was frequently affixed to a piece of tape on the gambler's finger, and honest players simply assumed he had suffered a minor cut and never gave the tape a second thought.

The most subtle method of marking honest cards was used by the punch man. This sharp wore an ordinary-looking finger ring on one hand, but projecting outwards from the underside of the ring was a needle point about one sixty-fourth of an inch long. When the cards were held in that hand the sharp would press the corner of a card against the point and raise a tiny bump on the opposite side of the card. A man with a sensitive touch could detect the tiny projection on the desirable cards and deal them to himself.

One female sharp used to wear an ornate antique brooch while playing cards, and when not actually looking at her cards she would hold them against her chest. The brooch had a sharp point concealed in the design and the lady used it to mark certain cards.

3. We come to the third, best and most successful class of professional gambler – the men who played in secret partnership with one or two confederates and used only honest cards without resorting to manipulation. (They did not need to, because no single player could hope to defeat a combination of players.) The reason for this was simple: with three sharps secretly allied against one victim, the odds were three to one against the mark. Simple, uninspired play was all that was necessary for the team of sharps to fleece the victim very soundly.

The critical requirement for a successful team of confederates was a secret code of signals that would allow the allied players to telegraph information back and forth to each other with the victim being none the wiser. Card values and suits held by each player became the common knowledge of the whole team, and this would determine how the team would play against the victim. The code consisted of subtle finger and hand movements and eventually became fairly standardised to facilitate its use among the fraternity.

Usually a team of sporting men would arrange to work together before the voyage began, but this was not always the case. A silent agreement could be arrived at during a game by two sharps who were not previously acquainted, and this was done in the following way.

One sharp would be engaged in a game with several potential victims, and a second sharp, having observed the play for a while, would know that the first gambler was working alone. When an opening presented itself, the newcomer would address the first sharp. 'Do you know Mr Hemingway, the one engaged in the rabbit business?' This was the newcomer's way of identifying himself as a fellow sharp in search of prey. 'Hemingway' was the hustler's code for a member of the profession, and, just to make certain there was no mistake, the 'rabbit business' meant 'this evening's victim'. If the first sharp answered affirmatively, he would then invite the newcomer to sit down and join the game, but a negative answer meant the first sharp intended to fleece the lambs by himself.

A separate set of subtle hand signals existed to serve the same purpose. While sitting down to a game, a newcomer would hold his open palm against his chest with thumb extended. This identified him as a member of the gambling fraternity in search of a confederate, and a sharp already seated at the table would then signal either 'welcome, brother' or 'these sheep are mine'. Once the confederates were playing the game and had opened the lines of communication, the odds of winning were heavily in their favour. Their victim, even if suspicious, would have no concrete proof that cheating was taking place.

Some teams of gamblers specialised in the game of poker, and the secret confederate technique was well suited to the game. For instance, the ally who held the strongest cards would be the only one to stay in the game, thus pitting the best hand of the allies against that of the mark. The victim did not become suspicious, because the winning was not confined to just one of his opponents.

In sitting down to a game, two sharps would contrive to sit on either side of a rich target. They could then resort to 'cross-firing', or raising their bets continuously no matter how weak their cards were. In order to stay in the game, the victim would have to match their bets, but eventually he would have to drop out and the two sharps could finish the hand any way they saw fit.

The lures of poker did not appeal to all teams of sharps, and some preferred to specialise in bridge whist. An Atlantic passage in first class provided wealthy victims as well as time to bilk them with the proper finesse, but there were a few drawbacks as well. Bridge whist was a game of skill where the better players figured to win and knew it. A victim would have to be a good player to get involved in a game for high stakes, so it was difficult to cheat the better players consistently because they recognised incongruous play. The team of sharps had to treat a dupe gingerly if they expected to get a proper return on their investment of time and money.

An account written in 1939 by Michael MacDougall outlined the classic plan used by three sharps preparing for an ocean bridge game. After targeting a potential victim in first class, one of three partners would quietly relieve him of his wallet and turn it over to the purser, contents intact. Upon returning the wallet to its owner, the purser would tell the victim who it was that had turned it in, and the grateful man would search out his benefactor to thank him. He would usually find the 'good Samaritan' in his cabin engaged in a three-handed bridge game, and naturally the three players (all of whom were professional card mechanics) would jovially invite the victim to sit in on a game. The mark would win moderately and would return the next day to play again with his new-found friends.

This routine would continue until the last day of the voyage, or perhaps even on the boat train after the ship had docked. The dupe had won moderately but consistently for the entire voyage and, by now, any suspicions he might have harboured were completely laid to rest. When the voyage was almost over (or before the boat train reached the end of the line), one of the sharps would suggest playing 'Mississippi style', where points could be redoubled indefinitely (and hence huge amounts of money would be involved). Play would run close for a while, but then one of the sharps would secretly 'ring in a cold deck' – a deck of cards that had been stacked so that the mark would receive an outstanding hand. (One of these hands was used so often it became known as the Mississippi Heart Hand.) The mark would be flushed with confidence and would encourage heavy betting, but of course the deck had been arranged so that one of the sharps received a better hand, and the mark lost very heavily. Usually he would be forced to write a cheque to cover his losses and, once the ship landed, the sharps would make a beeline for the bank to cash the cheque just in case the victim might suspect something was amiss and stop payment.

Sometimes the sharps would use the following ploy to ensure that payment on a cheque would not be stopped. One of the sharps would accept the cheque from the victim and pocket it, but would then feign an attack of conscience, produce the cheque from his pocket, tear it up and offer to settle for whatever money the victim had on him. Relieved at saving a fortune, the victim would hand over a couple of hundred dollars to settle his debt, but, unknown to him, the gambler had actually destroyed a blank check and secretly retained the good one. One can imagine the discomfiture of the victim when he saw the original cancelled cheque on his bank statement and realised he had been taken for his bank account as well as for all the cash he had been carrying on board the ship!

If a victim was prominent enough, a group of sharpers might occasionally trust him to mail the cheque to cover his losses. A group of hustlers once fleeced an Ohio senator at bridge on a train, and one of the gamblers gave the senator his New York address and told him to mail the cheque at his convenience. Later, after reflecting upon the game, the senator became convinced he had been cheated and asked the secret service to check that New York address. It turned out to be a cheap tenement that the gamblers used as a mail drop, so the senator tore up his cheque and philosophically wrote off his cash losses in the game.

The victim was Warren G. Harding, later the twenty-eighth president of the United States.

Captain Edward J. Smith, who later commanded the *Titanic*, was instrumental in hamstringing a team of nine 'Knights of the Card and Chip' during a February 1909 voyage of the White Star liner *Adriatic*. Soon after clearing Cherbourg during a westward crossing, Captain Smith was notified of the presence of these nine gamblers on board his ship and immediately ordered the 'Professional Gamblers on Board' signs to be posted in the card rooms to alert the passengers of their peril. Most of the grifters took the hint and exerted very little effort to relieve passengers of their superfluous cash, but three gamblers did lure two men into a small poker game and succeeded in mulcting them of $33. The fact that the gamblers spent $50 on refreshments during that game meant that, combined with the total cost of their individual passages, the nine sharps had expended about $1,400 in transportation costs while reaping an income of only $33.

2

THE NON-*TITANIC* PLAYERS

Before turning our attention to the gamblers who sailed on the *Titanic*, let us examine the careers of a number of confidence men whose names have been inextricably linked with that disaster even though they were never on board the doomed vessel. A synopsis of their careers (what little is known of them) should prove instructive in illustrating the type of men who actually sailed on the ship in hope of making a maiden voyage killing.

A young Harry Silberberg.

Harry Silberberg, alias John Silverton, 'Tricky' Silverton, Silverthorne and a dozen other pseudonyms, was known to the police on two continents as 'the world's greatest swindler'. He was equally good at crooked gambling, forgery and promoting investment schemes.

Silberberg, the son of a Jewish rabbi, was born in Atlanta, Georgia, and received a good education. While still fairly young he spent some time out west and learned to handle a deck of cards. While dabbling in Colorado politics, he was appointed commissioner to raise funds for the erection of a building at the World's Fair, but he quickly absconded with the funds to Chicago and then proceeded to Europe. In Venice he met a countess who, being convinced that Silberberg loved her, divorced her husband and followed the con man to Baden-Baden. There, Silberberg impersonated J. Coleman Drayton, once the son-in-law of William Astor (father of John Jacob Astor). Using this identity, he obtained 40,000 German marks' worth of diamonds on credit and promptly left with the countess for London. Confronted there by the real J. Coleman Drayton,

Silberberg was arrested and sent back to Baden-Baden, where he was convicted of swindling and deported as an undesirable.

Silberberg next went to Siam (now Thailand) and, using forged credentials, obtained a railroad-building concession from the king. He then forged the king's name to a $40,000 bank draft, cashed it and left for Calcutta (now Kolkata). Passing himself off there as a cousin of J. Coleman Drayton, he was royally entertained by the viceroy.

Silberberg's career continued to flourish after he returned to the United States, and he promoted land schemes in Mexico and Texas and, incidentally, married Clara Barklow of San Antonio. Silberberg occasionally travelled to New York or abroad, and he always gambled as he travelled.

The real J. Coleman Drayton was being driven to distraction by the knowledge that his good name was being used dishonestly. In Chicago a detective tipped off Drayton that Silberberg was in town, and once again the two men confronted one another. Silberberg had forged Drayton's name on a $500 bank draft that Drayton had then had to pay for, but, when accused of forgery, Silberberg maintained

Another photograph of the youthful Harry Silberberg.

that he too was a real Drayton. He calmly handed Drayton $500 and apologised for any inconvenience the confusion might have caused, and the mollified Drayton declined to press charges.

At another time Silberberg was posing as Drayton on an ocean liner that, by sheer chance, was also carrying the real Drayton. Hearing that his old nemesis was again using the Drayton name, J. Coleman Drayton repaired to Silberberg's stateroom, dragged him from his berth and administered a sound thrashing to the hapless con man.

In 1903 Silberberg arrived in Minneapolis and, calling himself J.J. DeBralls, opened a school of hypnotism. A Miss Heebner became his assistant and later purchased a partnership for $250. Meanwhile, on the other side of town, Silberberg assumed the identity of J.J. Carlisle, nephew of a New York millionaire and former Secretary of the Treasury. A few weeks after the 'DeBralls' hypnotism school opened, 'Carlisle' proposed to Miss Bonnie Hinkle and the two were married in St Paul. Silberberg then left on a business trip while keeping his dual existence secret.

Acting on Miss Heebner's complaint, the police arrested Silberberg in Washington DC and returned him to a Minneapolis jail. After his multiple identities were exposed, Mrs 'Carlisle' obtained a divorce from the con man.

When Silberberg began to waste away in jail a doctor pronounced him tubercular, so the sharp asked that bail be lowered to $1,000 so that he could move to a better climate. This request was granted, and a relative paid the required sum to free Silberberg. The con man promptly jumped bail, went to Chicago and lavishly entertained his friends at a hotel.

During the period Silberberg had been operating in Minneapolis he claimed to be a brother-in-law of Jacob Theriot, the American Consul in Portugal, but a cabled query to Lisbon brought a quick denial of this claim. Later, after the con man was released from jail, the consul sent a letter telling how, in 1897, Silberberg had been

Mug shot of a seasoned Harry Silberberg.

in a German prison for a diamond swindle and had asked Theriot for a pardon. The grifter had given every appearance of dying of tuberculosis at the time, so the pardon had been granted. (It turned out that Silberberg had a sensitive tooth that could be made to bleed at will, and the grifter was using this ploy to give the appearance of coughing up blood whenever it might be required.)

Silberberg's last well-publicised con took place in 1907 when he promoted a shipbuilding scheme in New York. He managed to interest many millionaires in the plan and was able to pocket $200,000 before his plans were exposed.

On top of everything else, Silberberg had plans to write a book about his exploits, and the stories he told to fascinated listeners were confirmed by police officials the world over. He was even rumoured to be the 'Greyhound' in a play of the same name written by Wilson Mizner; the play concerned the exploits of a successful confidence man, and Harry Silberberg could definitely be described as successful. The last the Pinkertons heard of him, Silberberg was financially secure and living in a villa somewhere in the Mediterranean.

Not long after the *Titanic* went down it was rumoured in New York that a large number of sporting men had been planning to book passage on the ill-fated vessel, and various New York grifters recalled the names of some of their colleagues. One gambler recalled speaking with 'Doc' Owen, who expressed his intention to make the *Titanic*'s maiden voyage. Owen boasted of hatching a brand-new con game whose target was to be no less a personage than John Jacob Astor. The success of the plan relied on the fact that Astor, being on his honeymoon, would be in his happiest and least suspicious frame of mind. The con artist did not go into detail, but he insisted the plan was 'a peach' and had an excellent chance of success.

Another of the sharps thought to be planning to return to America on the *Titanic* was Bud Hauser, whose death on the *Olympic* in 1912 we have already discussed. Hauser and 'Frankie' Dwyer were said to have sailed to England together for that purpose, but, when they arrived in Southampton, Hauser was reportedly taken aback by the large number of sporting men who were intending to make this maiden voyage. Rather than compete with his brethren for the limited number of marks, Hauser decided to return to America via an earlier ship – a course of action that would allow him a little elbow room at the card table. Hauser chose the *Olympic* and boarded her on 3 April, along with George McMullen and several other sharps. (It was rumoured that 'Frankie' Dwyer changed his mind at the last minute about accompanying Hauser on the *Olympic* and decided to sail on the *Titanic* after all, but – despite this rumour – it seems likely that Dwyer sailed on the *Olympic* along with his friends.)

It was later claimed that Tom McAuliffe was the leader of the band of grifters who travelled to England for the specific purpose of returning to the States on the *Titanic*'s maiden voyage. McAuliffe (known as 'One-armed Mac') briefly discussed his plans with another sharper who intended to remain behind in New York, and he said he was looking forward to the *Titanic*'s sailing and expressed the opinion that his band of con men would find 'easy pickings' among the 'boobs' on board the ship. The fact that McAuliffe had only one arm did not interfere with his skill at the card table, since it was said he used his one arm to better advantage than most of his colleagues used both of theirs. His disability was also an advantage in that his intended victim would think him incapable of cheating successfully. During his career, McAuliffe was said to have impersonated nearly every big businessman in the world.

James Gordon and William Day (also known as Jack Day) were two fellow members of McAuliffe's band, but no details are available concerning their backgrounds.

Ernest Jeffrey (known as 'Peaches' Van Camp) was another member of the gang. 'Peaches' was said to be a newcomer to the deep-water game, even though he was already an accomplished grifter on shore.

'Buffalo' Murphy was a fellow member of McAuliffe's band of grifters and was a steady ocean traveller during the spring and summer season who was planning to make the *Titanic*'s maiden voyage. Murphy was fond of travelling under the name of J.W. White, a chewing-gum magnate, and had sailed the North Atlantic steadily for the past fifteen years. Murphy was described as being one of the 'original street fair fakirs and an all-around skin game man'; he was notoriously thrifty with his money and was reportedly worth $200,000.

Al McPherson, another professional gambler, was reportedly invited to accompany the 'gang' to England to participate in the coming 'slaughter of the innocents', but he was a poor sailor and declined the invitation because of the awful bouts of seasickness he had experienced on two previous voyages.

The confidence man whose name is most widely associated with the *Titanic* disaster is Jay T. Yates, alias J.H. Rogers.

Jacob Yates was a wealthy livestock commission merchant in north-western Ohio, and, when his wife Barbara died in 1860, she left him with five daughters and two sons to raise. The father and children lived together for some time, but the responsibility of both raising and providing for his children must have been great. When Jacob met Mary Hook, their courtship eventually led to marriage and they had six children of their own: George, Barney, Jay (born 1 July 1867), Carrie, Fannie and Charles. Jacob Yates and his family lived on a farm south of Findlay, and it was there that the children grew up.

After Jay Yates was fully grown, his father gave him a valuable farm, apparently hoping his son would settle down there with his wife, the former Bessie Hanna Williams. Jay had other plans and, after moving into Findlay, he went to work as a hack driver for a local transfer line. This was only a temporary situation, though, because he was never able to hold a regular job for long. During this period, he was also said to have been in trouble with the Findlay police for numerous driver misdemeanours.

Jay Yates.

Before his death on 13 August 1896, Jacob Yates must have been apprehensive about the future of his son – and with good reason. Jay soon borrowed $1,900 on his farm by having a woman forge his wife's signature on the legal forms. During this same period he was indicted for forgery several times by the county grand jury, but the incidents were usually settled quietly by family and friends, and his mother spent a great deal of money getting her son out of his difficulties.

Men who knew Jay Yates in Findlay said he was an inveterate card player, and the last time he was seen by a certain friend in Findlay he was playing poker with a group of men; after losing one hand of cards Yates apparently drew a revolver, declared himself the winner and absconded with all the money.

Around 1902 Yates sold his farm and used the proceeds to leave Findlay and do a little travelling. Hanna Yates did not accompany her husband during his wanderings but remained at home. One report claims that she and Jay obtained a divorce in 1907, but this report is untrue. Hanna continued to hold her husband's life insurance policies and paid the premiums regularly, she having been named as the beneficiary.

Yates spent long periods of time away from home but would drop relatives an occasional postcard signed with his alias of J.H. Rogers. Sooner or later he always returned to his wife's home on West Pearl Street and, after he went to bed, Hanna would carefully go through his pockets. Sometimes Yates would be carrying very large sums of money, and Hanna would take some and put it away for a rainy day without him ever missing it. At other times her husband would return home flat broke, and Hanna would give him money for a new stake.

In the winter of 1909–10 Yates journeyed to Washington DC and spent a month or so at a prominent hotel. He was always well-dressed and, due to his smooth and pleasing personality, he made a lot of friends during that period. Yates did not spend his time in complete idleness, though, because he was formulating a scheme whereby some easy money would soon be coming his way.

On 7 January 1910 Yates walked into station 19, a post office sub-station at Third Street and Pennsylvania Avenue South-east, and showed a calling card identifying himself as a postal inspector. He was subsequently allowed to examine the accounts and soon discovered some 'irregularities' in certain money order blanks. After handing the superintendent a receipt, Yates left the substation with the money orders after announcing they would be turned in at headquarters. Less than two hours later, a real postal inspector arrived at the substation, at which time the ruse was discovered and two detectives were loosed upon his trail. Yates, however, managed to give them the slip.

From Washington DC, Yates returned to Ohio where he met with a wealthy cousin who lived in Columbus. He told this relative he had been working for the government on the Panama Canal and always carried his money in post office money orders for safety. The cousin knew that J.H. Rogers was not Yates's real name, but, after being assured that the alias was used for business purposes and that the endorsement was legitimate, he confirmed Yates's identity to a bank. Yates cashed twenty-seven $100 money orders at the Union National Bank and then left town; the unfortunate cousin was forced to repay the money to the government, and the postal authorities renewed their search for Jay Yates, alias J.H. Rogers.

Members of the Yates family recall another of Jay's escapades in which he used the very same ploy as the one outlined above. About 4 miles south of Findlay, beside the New York Central railroad tracks, was a small junction named Kirt Ellis. The place consisted of a small post office, handle factory, blacksmith shop and perhaps a few more small businesses. Yates arrived in town and, again posing as a postal inspector, got away with more postal bonds. Not long after Yates's departure the little post office closed and the town broke up. (Yates was probably not responsible for the demise of the little town, and it is uncertain whether this theft occurred before or after his Washington job.)

Dropping out of the limelight, Jay Yates began to spend time travelling to Europe and back on board the great ocean liners. He had always been an avid card player and seemed determined to make it his primary means of livelihood. Yates's postcards to his family became fewer and, in 1910, he wrote a last one to his mother from London before dropping out of sight for the next two years.

Yates's activities between 1910 and 1912 remain unknown beyond the fact that New York detectives were aware of his deep-water gambling activities. Around 1 February 1912, Yates dropped a postcard to his sister, Mrs Frank J. Adams of Findlay, that he mailed from New York City and signed with his alias J.H. Rogers. A Yates descendant reports that Jay also sent postcards to his wife Hanna telling her he planned to return home from England on the *Titanic*, but the family had no further news about Jay Yates until Mrs Adams was contacted by a New York newspaper two months later.

3

THE *TITANIC* GAMBLERS

As the time for the maiden voyage of the *Titanic* approached, anticipation rose among the 'gentlemen of the green cloth' who intended to sail with her. These sporting men knew that many men prominent in the business and social worlds would be attracted by the prospect of sailing on the world's largest and most luxurious ocean liner and would be making this crossing to New York. And so, as the end of March 1912 grew near, a group of American sharpers left New York for England for the express purpose of booking their return passage on the *Titanic*. New York hotel detectives were aware of at least six well-known gamblers making up this band, and they probably wondered what kind of success would attend these sharps during the return voyage.

Once the band reached England, the grifters had about ten days to kill before the *Titanic*'s sailing date. It is not known how the sharps spent this interval, but some of them probably attempted to redistribute some of England's wealth by means of either a well-turned card or by one of the short con games the Americans were so good at.

At least five professional gamblers booked first-class passages on the *Titanic*'s maiden voyage and bought their tickets together, but at the very last minute two of these men changed their minds and joined gambler 'John Killinger' on board the *Celtic*, which departed Southampton on 11 April and arrived in New York on 20 April. The two gamblers who changed their minds were using the aliases 'Anthony Melody' and 'J.M. White', and they transferred their bookings so late that their names remained on the *Titanic*'s first-class passenger list that was distributed on board on sailing day. (It is possible 'J.M. White' was in truth 'Buffalo' Murphy, a gambler who often travelled using the name of J.W. White, a chewing-gum magnate.)

Despite all the rumours that a large gang of grifters boarded the *Titanic* on sailing day, only three card sharps actually did so – George Brereton, Charles Romaine and Harry Homer.

GEORGE A. BRERETON

George Brereton was born on 12 November 1874 in Medelia, Minnesota, his father having come from Ireland and his mother Mary from Bavaria. George had four brothers (Clarence, Frank, John and William) as well as two sisters (Emily and May).

George Brereton.

In 1880, the national census recorded young George Brereton and his family as still living in Medelia, but by 1895 the family had moved to Minneapolis. The 1900 census shows the family living at 608 16th Avenue South, Minneapolis, but it also shows that George was no longer listed as living with his parents.

Nothing is known of Brereton's life and activities between 1901 and 1910, by which time he was 36 years old and listed as working as a waiter in a restaurant in St Paul, Minnesota. Researcher Mike Herbold has determined that, at various points in his life, Brereton claimed to be head of a manufacturing concern, a merchant, real estate agent, builder, contractor, president of a finance company, retired, a car salesman and a retired real estate broker. It is very unlikely that any of these claims were true, but it is known with certainty that Brereton had a crooked streak a mile long.

Among the members of the gambling fraternity, Brereton was known as 'Boy' Bradley, George Bradley, Ralph Bradley, George Braden, George A. Brayton, George A. Banning, et al. Brereton seems to have spent a great deal of time travelling on passenger liners. On 26 July 1911 he boarded the new White Star liner *Olympic* (commanded by Captain Edward J. Smith) in New York and arrived in Southampton on 2 August. Even though professional gamblers customarily used aliases on such occasions, George A. Brereton was using his real name when he reboarded the *Olympic* at Southampton on 9 August 1911 and arrived back in New York on 16 August. Brereton again used his own full name on 12 September 1911 when he boarded the German liner *Kaiser Wilhelm der Grosse* at Southampton and arrived in New York on 19 September. (A man named 'John Logsdon' was travelling in company with Brereton, 'J.H. Logsdon' being an alias of fellow gambler Harry Homer.) After 19 September 1911, George Brereton seems to have stopped using his real name on ships' passenger lists and resorted to using aliases.

On 9 March 1912, 'George Bradley' (in company with his friend Harry Homer) sailed from Liverpool on the *Lusitania* and arrived in New York on 15 March 1912. He apparently boarded another ship for England within a very few days, because April 1912 found Brereton in Southampton preparing to use his 'George Bradley' alias when he boarded the new White Star liner *Titanic* on 10 April.

CHARLES HALLACE ROMAINE

The second of *Titanic*'s three card sharps was Charles Romaine, known to his colleagues as 'Harry' Romaine, C.H. Romaine, C. Rolmane, C.H. Romacue and C.H. Rotheld.

Charles 'Harry' Romaine.

Charles Romaine was born in Georgetown, Kentucky, on 11 July 1866 and was one of twelve children of farmer William Romine and his wife Julia, he being the youngest son. (The spelling of the family name differed from person to person.) When his father died in 1867, his mother was remarried to farm labourer Joshua Secrist, who had several children of his own. The 1880 census listed Charles as 'Harrison Sechrest', who was working as a labourer in Oliver, Ohio. Around 1892 the family moved to Anderson, Indiana, where Charles became associated with George Simmons in managing the Hotel Doxey. Around 1895 Charles Romaine married Eileen Doll (born 15 March 1874) and lived with her in Anderson until at least 1905.

It seems likely that Charles and Doll Romaine moved to New York sometime prior to 1907, because during that year he began to make occasional ocean voyages to Europe. On 1 November 1907, travelling under an alias, 'Charles Rolmane' arrived in New York from Southampton on the White Star liner *Adriatic*. On 19 November 1909 he arrived in New York from Le Havre, France, on *La Provence*, this time using his own name on the passenger list.

By 1910 Romaine and his wife were living at West 109th Street in New York City, where he reportedly earned his living as a stock-broker.

On 24 February 1911 Romaine again booked an ocean passage using his real name and arrived in New York from Liverpool on the Cunard liner *Lusitania*. His mother passed away in April 1911, but he and his wife continued to live in New York City for the next twelve months.

HARRIS WILLIAM HAVEN HOMER

The third of *Titanic*'s bunco men was Harris Homer, who preferred to be called 'Harry' but was known to his peers as 'Kid' Homer, George Homer, Henry Stevens, H. Haven, Harry Baldwin, C.H. Brewster, J.H. Logsdon, et al. (It should be noted that 'Logsdon' was his sister's married name.)

Harry 'Kid' Homer in his prime.

In truth, we know very little about Harry Homer's career, and it seems likely that, in order to prevent embarrassment to his family, he told them only what he wanted them to believe.

Harry's father, Dr Richard Homer, came to the United States from Dudley, England, and practised medicine in Covington, Kentucky, until 1864, at which time he moved to Knightstown, Indiana. Dr Homer was a highly esteemed citizen in Knightstown, and it was there that Harry was born on 28 November 1871 and where he grew up with his four surviving brothers (William, Charlie, Richard and Morris) and his four surviving sisters (Lizzie, Mary, Louise and Lillie). In 1880 the census listed the family as residing in Knightstown, Indiana.

On 9 March 1893, 21-year-old Harry Homer and 18-year-old Delia Atwater (born 1875) were married in Chicago, and in 1904 the young couple had a daughter named Ruth. Unfortunately, not much else is known about this union or how long it lasted.

A young Harry Homer, *c.*1875.

Harry Homer as a young man.

By the turn of the century Homer seems to have got off to a good start as a confidence man, because, on 12 April 1900, the *Chicago Inter Ocean* reported the following:

> James Mulligan and Harry Homer, who were arrested a few days ago on a charge of swindling Thomas Corwin out of $300 by means of a confidence game, were held to the Criminal court by Justice Prindiville yesterday. Mulligan is the man who played the part of a detective when two of his companions secured nearly $13,000 from W. L. Bennett, the 'get-rich-quick' man who recently decamped.

Homer's father died in 1902, and Harry was subsequently listed as making his living as a 'cattleman'. This claim was probably untrue, because on New Year's Day in 1902, the following article (possibly about 'our' Harry Homer) appeared in the *New York Sun* regarding incidents that took place in Cleveland, Ohio, the day before:

> Two alleged confidence men were arrested by Patrolmen Wood and Weisbarth at the Union station at 10:30 a.m. today. Jacob J. Robin, a gas mantle manufacturer of New York, told this story at Central Station half an hour before the arrest.
>
> 'I am stopping at the Colonial Hotel, and last night I met two strangers who were so congenial that we had several drinks together. One of the strangers, who said his name was Max Cohen, looked at a man in the rear of the barroom and turning to me, said: "There's a jolly good fellow. I want to fool him; let me take your ring a second." I gave him my gold ring and he went into the lavatory. That's the last I saw of Max Cohen or the jolly good fellow.'
>
> Wood and Weisbarth went to the station and found the men buying tickets. Cohen dashed out of the train shed, followed by Wood, who caught him at the top of the Seneca street hill. Weisbarth attended to the other man, who said he was Harry Homer of Boston.

On 8 April 1902 the *Akron Daily Democrat* printed a cryptic little notice that might possibly have been referring to 'our' Harry Homer:

> Harry Homer of Megadore, and Howard Fritch of Akron, were in town Saturday evening at the office of G.W. Fritch Esq. on official business, and no doubt by this time Constable Royer is serving a warrant.

Homer's criminal career continued to blossom during the next five years, because on 26 August 1901 (under his alias 'Harry H. Dillon') he was arraigned for suspicious activity in Buffalo, New York, and was given just twenty-four hours to leave the city. On 30 December of that same year, Homer (under his own name) was arraigned in Cleveland, Ohio, on a charge of grand larceny but was discharged in police court on 3 January 1902. On 14 December 1905 he was arraigned under his own name for loitering in Cincinnati, and two days later he was fined $50 plus court costs. In Hot Springs, Arkansas, Homer (under his alias 'Harry Dillon') was arraigned on 24 April 1906 but was discharged (although it was noted he was a 'pal' of criminals Chappy Moran, M.H. Munk, A.J. Poigndexter, Thomas Gleason and Frank Smith). During this same time period police noted the fact that Homer was 34 years old, 5ft 9in tall, 180lb in weight and of medium and stout build. He had blue eyes, sandy hair and a florid complexion, with a mole above his left eyebrow and several tattoos.

On 4 July 1906, it was reported that a series of robberies had recently taken place in Hot Springs, Arkansas, and 'gamblers, pickpockets and crooks of all classes have been plying their trades in Hot Springs and escaped criminals have been overlooked by the police'. One such criminal was Harry Homer, 'a noted pickpocket whose picture is in every rogues' gallery in the country, and especially in the East'. Homer was stopping at a leading hotel in the city and was

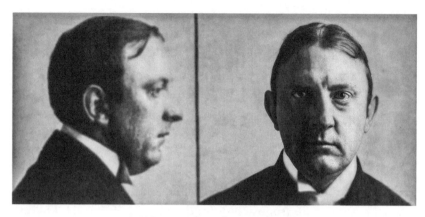

A 1906 mug shot of Harry Homer.

thought to have committed some of these crimes without being arrested for them, the money involved ranging from $35 to $1,800 in just the previous thirty days. Among the dozen crimes committed within the past three weeks were:

(1) W.L. Helfin, Moulton, Arkansas, robbed of $600 in a gambling house at the point of a pistol.
(2) Jule Billot, Bonnonts, Montana, $1,800 in a similar manner.
(3) W.H. Mills, Henry County, Alabama, $35 in a blind tiger game.
(4) Henry Hasbrough, Malvern, Arkansas, $325 and railroad tickets by pickpockets.
(5) James R. Day, cheques for $16.80, but stopped payment in time to prevent cashing.
(6) R.L. Pullen, Evergreen, Alabama, $160 by confidence men.

It seems likely that Homer was involved in the above-mentioned confidence games and pickpocketing schemes rather than participating in the outright robberies, but there was a push in Hot Springs to form a vigilance committee and the city council was called into special session to get to grips with the crime wave.

In November 1908 Homer found himself in New Orleans, Louisiana, at a time when officials there were doing their best to quash illegal gambling in their city. A local newspaper described what happened next:

Detectives Mooney and Holyland yesterday afternoon arrested James L. Wright and Harry H. Homer, said to be well-known to the police, and locked them up in the First Precinct Police Station, where they were charged with being dangerous and suspicious characters. Very little money was found on either of the prisoners when searched, [and] it is the supposition of the detectives that they had come to recuperate financially. Homer is said to have had his picture in the local rogue's gallery, and has been arrested in various cities in connection with wire-tapping, pocket-picking and other alleged crooked work. When seen last night, Wright said he was merely passing through New Orleans on his way to Cuba, and Homer [was] emphatic in declaring that he had stopped off only a few hours while en route to San Antonio, Texas.

From early childhood Homer and his sister Louise were very close, and this special relationship continued even after he left home. According to Louise, her brother travelled for a land company in Texas and his duties carried him all over the country as well as to Europe. Homer was said to have important investments in Denver, being involved with a realty company there and also promoting the Denver National Stock Exchange Corporation. He was travelling most of the time but always kept in touch with Louise, who by this time had married and moved to Indianapolis. Homer made his sister's home his headquarters, received his mail there and made many friends in the city during his brief visits.

By 1911 Homer seems to have begun using aliases whenever he travelled at sea. One such alias was 'J.H. Logsdon', since using his sister Louise's married name made it easy for him to remember. On 12 September 1911 'John Logsdon' boarded the German liner *Kaiser Wilhelm der Grosse* at Southampton and arrived in New York on 19 September. ('Logsdon' was travelling in company with gambler George Brereton.) On 20 October 1911 'John Logsdon' again arrived in New York, this time from La Havre, on board the liner *La Provence*.

In February 1912 Homer left the United States on (supposedly) a pleasure trip to Europe, it being his fourth trip abroad in the past year. One of Homer's announced goals was to visit the birthplace of his father in Dudley, England, and in March of that year his sister Louise Logsdon received word that he was in Cairo, Egypt. (In reality, Homer was travelling as 'Henry Homer' when he and fellow grifter George Brereton boarded the *Lusitania* in Liverpool on 9 March and arrived back in New York on 15 March.)

There was no further word of Harry Homer until after the *Titanic* went down.

4

ON BOARD THE *TITANIC*

On 10 April 1912, gamblers George Brereton and Charles Romaine were preparing to board the *Titanic* at Southampton as first-class passengers, but their names were not listed as such on the ship's passenger list; on this voyage, George Brereton was staying in cabin B-100 under the alias 'George Brayton', while Charles Romaine booked his own passage under the name 'C. Rolmane'. Just before boarding the *Titanic* one of the gamblers apparently sent a cable to a colleague in New York informing him of the ship's impending departure and asking him to meet them at the White Star pier with

two taxicabs when the ship completed her voyage. After accomplishing this final task, the gamblers went on board the great liner. It was almost noon. Sailing time had come.

The tugs began to ease *Titanic* away from the dock, the great engines began to turn over and she was underway, but in a matter of moments the long-awaited voyage was almost aborted before it even began. As the *Titanic* moved past the moored liners *Oceanic* and *New York* the water being displaced by her movement caused the *New York* to strain at her mooring lines; suddenly they gave way, and the *New York*'s stern swung out into the channel towards the mammoth liner. Quick work by *Titanic*'s tugs narrowly averted a collision and, after a brief delay, the big liner resumed her voyage. George Brereton and Charles Romaine undoubtedly breathed a huge sigh of relief when the ship finally reached the open sea.

RMS *Titanic* departs Southampton on her maiden voyage.

At about 6 p.m. the *Titanic* reached Cherbourg, France, where she took on more passengers and mail. It was there that Harry Homer came aboard, having booked his passage on the vessel using the alias 'H. Haven'.

From Cherbourg the *Titanic* headed through the night for Ireland. Late on the morning of 11 April she reached Queenstown (now Cobh), where more passengers came aboard. Finally, shortly before 2.30 p.m., *Titanic* raised her anchor for the very last time. Then, turning slowly towards the west, her engines began that relentless, monotonous pounding that swiftly carried her away from the Irish coast and out onto the vast expanse of the North Atlantic.

Most passengers spent the first day of the maiden voyage getting settled in, looking up old friends and becoming familiar with one's table acquaintances. After surrounding oneself with a congenial circle of companions, a passenger could begin to establish a daily routine: a swim in the pool, a brisk walk on deck or a game of squash beckoned invitingly, or one might relax in a deck chair and chat with friends or possibly choose a book from the ship's well-stocked library. Evenings in first class were an opportunity to enjoy an excellent meal and to mingle with one's peers in the social world. After dinner the ladies might gather in the Café Parisien to exchange the latest news concerning family and friends, while the men would often retire to the first-class smoking room for a cigar and some masculine conversation. The *Titanic* was carrying a large number of men who were of decided importance in political and business circles, and this fact alone ensured that there would be conversations worth listening to. The smoking room was also a fine location for a man to settle down at a table to enjoy an evening of poker or bridge whist; there always seemed to be at least one game in progress, and many men welcomed the opportunity to exercise their skill with the pasteboards.

Our band of three sharpers undoubtedly made good use of their time during the early days of the voyage, and the grifters probably attempted to insert themselves into various groups of receptive passengers. This tactic would be preparatory to the regular nightly card games in which, hopefully, their new acquaintances would participate. Eventually the gamblers succeeded in their efforts.

Time passed and, with each new day, the *Titanic's* speed gradually increased. The ship was performing beautifully, and passengers and crew were well satisfied with this brand-new addition to the White Star Line's stable of thoroughbreds.

On the evening of 13 April, a sour note was introduced into the thus-far pleasant shipboard activity when a poker game was arranged that was to include Henry B. Harris, the theatrical manager. It is possible that author Jacques Futrelle, Emil Brandeis and several other men participated in the game as well, but among these card players was included at least one of our 'gentlemen of the green cloth'.

Henry B. Harris.

The poker game proceeded normally for some time, but then things began to go wrong for the sharp. It is unlikely that the other players actually saw him executing a sleight with the cards, but possibly he became a little careless about the frequency with which he was winning. In any case, suspicion arose in the mind of Henry Harris that our man was a card mechanic. Nothing was said about it at the time, but the game probably broke up earlier than it would have done otherwise. This suspicion of cheating was to seriously hamper the sharp's efforts to make a killing before the end of the voyage, because word quickly spread among the passengers that the man was a suspected cheat and it was advisable not to play cards with him.

Despite the ill luck that befell this sharp, gambling coups were apparently being scored elsewhere on the North Atlantic. Early on the morning of 14 April a wireless message crackled into the *Titanic*'s Marconi room that was sent from the *Amerika* for retransmission by the *Titanic* and Cape Race. The message was addressed to a Louis Meyer of Los Angeles and was very brief and to the point:

NO SEASICKNESS. ALL WELL. NOTIFY ALL INTERESTED POKER BUSINESS GOOD.

AL

News of the success of a comrade-in-arms probably would have given scant comfort to the suspected sharp on the *Titanic*, because by the time luncheon was served on 14 April, his prospects for success were already beginning to dry up. When Henry Harris and his wife Renée finished dining with friends, an afternoon poker game was proposed, and Harris asked his wife if she would consent to be the eighth player should it become necessary. He then explained about the suspected sharp and said that, rather than bar him from the game, it would be simpler to let him see that the table was full.

Renée Harris.

Harris then pointed out the gambler, who was presently seated across the dining room from them, and Renée Harris was struck by the man's upstanding appearance and later recalled that he could have been 'a minister of the gospel, he looked so virtuous'. Renée agreed to participate in the card game, and an enjoyable afternoon was had by all. The sharp's carefully nurtured victims had just slipped from his grasp.

Down in the ship's steerage quarters at least one third-class passenger was becoming uneasy about all the gambling that had been taking place during the *Titanic*'s maiden voyage. Elizabeth Dowdell recalled later:

There was open gambling aboard the *Titanic* every day. No effort was made to conceal it. Even on Sunday the tables were crowded with men of the first and second cabins, and the games were open to anyone who wished to enter. I felt then that something dreadful would happen.

Jacques Futrelle.

The afternoon of 14 April wore on and, when a bugle was sounded at mealtime, the poker game broke up as the participants repaired to their staterooms to dress for dinner. Mr and Mrs Harris abandoned their poker game to do the same but, as she was descending the grand staircase, Renée Harris slipped and fell down the stairs, breaking her arm. The couple repaired to their stateroom where, after consultation with two doctors, her arm was placed in a cast.

Shortly thereafter, Mr and Mrs Harris entered the *Titanic*'s à la carte restaurant on B deck and sat down with their table companions, novelist Jacques Futrelle and his wife May. May Futrelle later commented on the atmosphere of that evening's dinner: the jewels and gowns worn by the ladies, the splendid examples of Edwardian manhood, the playing of the ship's orchestra, the sweet aroma of the roses at their table, the general air of good fellowship. Mr Harris and Mr Futrelle discussed the latest plays on the American stage, and they sat late at their table enjoying the good company of their friends.

May Futrelle.

Only one subject of conversation clouded the general good mood, and that was when the talk turned to the suspected professional gambler. The men again warned each other about the grifter and agreed to avoid engaging him in any card games.

By this time the situation seems to have worsened considerably for the sharp, since May Futrelle later recalled that he was shunned by almost everyone. The sharp's reputation had become general knowledge among the first-class passengers, and even his own table companions spoke to him only when the diktats of good breeding made it absolutely necessary. When the sharp was pointed out to May Futrelle, his outward appearance struck her quite differently than it had Renée Harris, because she saw him gazing over the crowd in the dining room with 'a cold, calculating smile' on his face. With his plans for a poker coup in ruins, the sharp may have been sizing up some different victims for a new game in the smoking room. Perhaps tonight it would be bridge whist.

Bridge games were commencing in several parts of the ship on the night of 14 April. After the evening meal was concluded, Miss Dorothy Gibson and her mother went to the first-class lounge on A deck and met Fred Seward and William Sloper, and the four passengers sat down to their game. After his wife retired for the evening, Lucien Smith joined sculptor Paul Chevré, cotton broker Alfred Omont and aviator Pierre Maréchal for a game in the Café Parisien, the three Frenchmen apparently enjoying the room's Gallic atmosphere.

But the three professional gamblers set their sights on the first-class smoking room, being well aware that many prominent men would gravitate there during the course of the evening. The sharps were after big game.

The first-class smoking room as it was on *Titanic* and her elder sister *Olympic*.

The first-class smoking room was situated at the aft end of *Titanic's* promenade deck. It was a large room, its length and width both being over 60ft, but its thick carpeting, upholstered leather furniture and dark mahogany panelling made it a very cosy place to spend a chilly evening. At one end of the room was a large open fireplace over which hung a large painting by Norman Wilkinson, *Entrance to Plymouth Harbour*. The side windows were of stained glass, upon which were depicted scenes of ancient ships, landscapes and other subjects. The light entering through these windows added further warmth and richness to an already magnificent room. The atmosphere was decidedly masculine, an air that the conversation, card playing, quiet laughter and aroma of good cigars only enhanced.

Many men took advantage of the smoking room as an excellent place to bring their day to a close. William Carter of Philadelphia was there along with Major Archibald Butt, chief military aide to President William Howard Taft. Seated at the same card table with Mr Carter and Major Butt were bibliophile Harry Widener and Clarence Moore, the master of hounds at a Washington hunt club. These four gentlemen were deeply intent on their own game of bridge.

William Dulles was there for a time, as was Edwin Kimball, manager of a Boston piano company. Colonel Archibald Gracie arrived early in the evening accompanied by his two friends, James Clinch Smith and Edward Kent, but Gracie was fatigued from his day's activities and retired early to his stateroom for some much-needed rest.

Shortly after 9 p.m. Major Arthur Peuchen arrived and, spying fellow Canadians Thomson Beattie and Thomas McCaffrey, went over to join them. The three men smoked and chatted, relaxing in each other's company. Soon Mr and Mrs Harris entered the room. Because Renée Harris's injured arm was set in a cast, she was wearing a sleeveless dinner dress; before long she grew chilly, so her husband escorted her from the smoking room in search of a warmer location.

Howard Case.

It is uncertain exactly when George Brereton, Charles Romaine and Harry Homer made their appearance in the smoking room, but it was probably shortly after the evening meal was concluded. The three grifters were planning to work together to entice an unwary victim into a game of bridge whist.

The three gamblers seem to have decided that Romaine would act as the 'outside man' for the evening, and it would be his job to befriend a victim and 'steer' him to the crooked card game where the entire team could deal with him properly. While Romaine was out in search of quarry, Brereton and Homer probably sat in the smoking room and played cards between themselves to while away the time until a prospective mark appeared on the horizon.

Romaine was attired in evening clothes as he stood out on the promenade deck viewing the dark waters as they slid by 60ft below. After a time, he was able to strike up a conversation with Howard Case, who was travelling for the Vacuum Oil Company. Soon the two men began to feel chilly, a highball was suggested, and Romaine accompanied Case along the deck to the smoking room. After obtaining their refreshment the two men probably sat down at the

Virginia Clark.

card table with Brereton and Homer. After chatting a while over their drinks, a bridge game was apparently suggested and someone produced a deck of cards.

Meanwhile, down in the first-class lounge, Virginia Clark of Los Angeles was chatting with Miss Edith Rosenbaum when, at about 9.30 p.m., she looked up to see her husband approaching. Clark told his wife he intended to go up to the smoking room to play bridge, and Virginia Clark replied, 'Play all the bridge you want, but under no circumstances do I want you to come down and wake me. I want to have a good night's sleep.'

After receiving his wife's permission to spend a 'night out with the boys', Walter Clark headed upstairs and walked along the promenade deck. Upon entering the smoking room in search of bridge opponents, Clark was apparently unable to find a game in need of a fourth player. Hoping, perhaps, to fill a vacant seat if one presented itself, Clark seems to have looked around the room in search of a game already in progress. He found one and, pulling up a chair, seated himself at the table with Howard Case and the three sharps.

Walter Clark.

(Charles Romaine later told of being seated at a table with both Howard Case and Walter Clark but did not mention they were playing cards; Harry Homer did say he was playing cards with Howard Case, but George Brereton was very reticent about identifying his bridge partners, saying, 'I would rather not mention the names of the party.') The fact that Clark was an alcoholic and was drunk that evening must have caused the three professional gamblers to welcome him with open arms, since an intoxicated mark often bet more recklessly at the card table than did a sober opponent who was observant and played with caution.

It appears that the three grifters were doing their best to establish themselves among a coterie of well-fixed people who enjoyed playing bridge. Once a routine was established, the sharps could then single out the passenger who seemed to make the easiest target. Later, as the voyage neared its conclusion, they could engage him in a game alone and fleece him in the prescribed manner. The three bunco men were probably at their charming best that night, anxious to gain the goodwill of their new acquaintances.

The evening wore on and, as the hour grew late, Romaine became aware that the *Titanic* was travelling more rapidly than ever. Basing his calculations on the previous day's speed, he concluded that the ship was making about 22 knots. He remarked to Case, 'How easy it is to tell that they are shoving this boat. I guess they can get us into New York by Tuesday night.' The men felt the ship's officers would like their brand-new vessel to make a record crossing on this maiden voyage.

Oblivious to the ship's increased speed, tennis champion Karl Behr was seated nearby in the smoking room. Behr had decided to stay up late and was talking with Richard Beckwith, with whose family Behr was travelling to the United States.

A three-handed card game was in progress at another table. One of the players, Alfred Nourney, was a tall German youth who hoped to land a job with an American auto manufacturer demonstrating

Bridge whist in *Titanic*'s smoking room.

their high-speed machines. Seated across the table from Nourney were furrier William Greenfield and Henry Blank, a New Jersey jeweller. As they played cards, the three men conversed quietly together in German while Blank enjoyed a final cigar of the evening.

Deeply engrossed in their own conversation were three other men sitting in nearby easy chairs. Charles C. Jones was superintendent of an estate in Vermont, while Algernon Barkworth was an English justice of the peace. Arthur Gee was on his way to Mexico City to take a job as manager of a linen mill. The three men had met only a few days before but had struck up quite a friendship in that brief time, and tonight they were discussing the science of good road-building, a subject in which Barkworth was keenly interested. It was growing late, though, and Barkworth began thinking about retiring until someone said that the ship's clock would be set back at midnight, so he decided to stay up until then and set his watch to the correct time.

Other men were not inclined to stay up that late. John B. Thayer, vice president of the Pennsylvania Railroad, stayed in the smoking room for a while, but then headed down to his stateroom and bed.

Spencer Silverthorne.

81

At about 11.20 p.m. Major Peuchen bade goodnight to his friends and retired, as did Edwin Kimball, Karl Behr and Richard Beckwith. A few minutes later Hugh Woolner and Mauritz Björnström-Steffanson, a lieutenant in the Swedish Artillery Guard, entered the smoking room along with two or three other night owls. The two men seated themselves and may have been joined by Colonel Gracie's two friends, Clinch Smith and Edward Kent. Woolner ordered a hot whisky and water from the bar, the others ordering similar hot drinks to stave off the chill of the night air.

Spencer Silverthorne, a buyer for a St Louis department store, might have been the only solitary figure in the smoking room as he sat reading in an easy chair while half-observing the progress of a nearby game of bridge whist in which several professional gamblers were participating. Silverthorne noted that one of the players (perhaps Charles Romaine) was an acquaintance with whom he had shared a recent voyage on the *Olympic* when the vessel dropped one of her propeller blades. Silverthorne peacefully reflected on that memory as he listened to the bridge players laughing and chatting over their card game and, as he glanced up at the ship's clock and checked his own watch, he saw it was exactly 11.39 p.m., 14 April 1912.

Suddenly the peaceful atmosphere of the smoking room was interrupted. Hugh Woolner later recalled it as a heavy grinding shock, felt rather than heard, that seemed to come from far ahead in the bows of the ship and then pass along the side of the vessel before dying away under their feet. At the same time the entire room seemed to shift, as if the *Titanic* had been pushed slightly to one side. According to one of the three sharps, 'The ship seemed to stop quickly, like a ferry boat going into a slip.'

Hugh Woolner immediately stood up, as did many other men in the smoking room who were looking around at each other in puzzlement. Spencer Silverthorne glanced at his acquaintance at the bridge table and said, 'Guess we've lost another propeller.' The man laughed at this little joke, but Silverthorne got up and headed outside to have a look around.

As Silverthorne stepped outside onto the promenade deck, he became one of the few people on board to actually see what was happening to the *Titanic*. A mountain of ice, so close it could almost be touched, was gliding silently along the ship's starboard side, scraping occasionally against the railing as it passed. Silverthorne watched the iceberg for fully a minute as, illuminated by the ship's lights, it passed slowly astern of the vessel and faded again into the blackness of the night.

In a moment Alfred Nourney, Henry Blank and William Greenfield stepped outside to see what had happened, as did William Carter and Algernon Barkworth. As Hugh Woolner and Mauritz Björnström-Steffanson reached the deck they heard a man exclaim, 'I just saw an iceberg 50ft higher than the top deck go by.' A few other men and women drifted towards the group standing outside the smoking room and made enquiries about the disturbance. No iceberg was visible now, but many eyes peered out into the darkness in an attempt to glimpse it. The *Titanic*'s engines had ceased to turn, but the ship was still making headway through the water and the chilly breeze sweeping along the deck tended to discourage lengthy conversation.

Since there seemed to be so little to see on deck, many men returned to the warmth of the smoking room to resume their interrupted activities. 'I went back in the smoking room with the others,' Spencer Silverthorne reported later. 'One of the bridge players had not left the smoking room at all and was waiting impatiently for the others to come back and resume the game. They returned and took up their hands.'

Major Butt, Clarence Moore, William Carter and Harry Widener resumed their bridge game, but many men had not bothered to get up from the card tables at all and continued their games while the others went on deck to investigate. George Brereton, Charles

Romaine and Harry Homer were among the imperturbable players who never went outside. 'When the ship struck the iceberg there was only a very slight impact,' one of the sharps (probably Brereton) recalled later. 'We joked at the thought of the *Titanic*'s going down and after a second resumed our poker game.'

A few other passengers were not quite so complacent. Mr Woolner and Lieutenant Björnström-Steffanson went off in search of Helen Churchill Candee, to whom Woolner had offered his services at the beginning of the voyage. After mingling with the group on deck for a while, Alfred Nourney decided to go below to do a little investigating. Perhaps, he thought, he could discover for himself if anything was really the matter.

Fred Seward stepped inside the smoking room for a moment, having felt the collision and come up from his stateroom in search of information. Seward noticed Howard Case seated nearby and questioned him about what had happened. 'I guess we've lost another propeller,' Case replied jokingly, 'but there is a compensation in that, as it will give us more time for bridge.' Apparently, Case was still seated at the card table with Walter Clark and the three sharps.

Presently one of the ship's officers appeared in the smoking room and told those present that the ship had struck ice but there was no danger, and the *Titanic* was again underway. Indeed, the great engines could be felt turning over slowly, so, since there was apparently no cause for alarm, the men in the smoking room dismissed the occurrence from their minds. Even so, William Carter bade his friends goodnight and went down to his stateroom to check on his wife and two children.

Walter Clark was still seated at the card table with Howard Case and the three sharps when he glanced towards the door of the smoking room and spied his wife's face peering anxiously in at him. Arising and going outside, Clark learned that his wife had just retired to her stateroom when she felt the collision and, looking out of the porthole, saw what she thought was a ship passing close beside the *Titanic*. She had become curious and, after dressing again, decided to consult her husband. Walter Clark told his wife he had felt the collision too but paid little attention to it. He related the officer's explanation and assured his wife that there was no cause for alarm, pointing out that the ship was moving again. Feeling reassured, Virginia Clark decided to remain on deck for another fifteen or twenty minutes and began conversing with several other passengers who were standing about. Her husband, meanwhile, returned to his bridge game, which continued at full tilt.

Shortly afterwards the doors of the smoking room were pushed open and Alfred Nourney returned. He hurried over to his friends Henry Blank and William Greenfield and began conversing excitedly in German. Nourney related how he had gone deep down into the ship and finally arrived at the squash court on G deck. It was deserted and, unbelievably, the floor was covered by 6in of green seawater. Greenfield was inclined to discount the story, perhaps thinking the young man was excitable, but Nourney asserted that his story was true and insisted that his friends accompany him back down to see for themselves. The three men left the smoking room to have a look. (Only fifteen minutes had elapsed since Nourney's first visit, but by the time the three men reached the squash court the water covering the floor was 6ft deep and rising steadily.)

Virginia Clark finished conversing with her friends outside the smoking room and went below to C deck and had almost reached her stateroom when she met a man coming towards her wearing a lifebelt. She laughed at him and said, 'Well, you must be a pretty nervous man', but he looked at her gravely and said that all passengers had been ordered to don lifebelts and assemble on the boat deck. Taken aback, she hurried back up to the smoking room and informed her husband. Together, the Clarks left the card room and went down to their stateroom to dress in warmer clothing.

This, in all likelihood, was the first hint of danger that the three professional gamblers received. Even so, it appears that Howard Case and the sharps were not impressed by Virginia Clark's story because, as George Brereton said later, 'We played bridge for three quarters of an hour after the *Titanic* struck the iceberg.' As the bridge game continued, Brereton could hear the ship's orchestra begin playing 'Alexander's Ragtime Band'.

In a nearby public room Mr and Mrs Futrelle stood with many other couples. Everyone wore lifebelts and awaited instructions, the wives staying very close to their husbands. The orchestra had just begun to play 'Alexander's Ragtime Band' when a group of stokers, fresh from the depths of the ship, burst into the brightly lit room and clustered together for a moment in one corner. Their faces were grimy with coal dust, but May Futrelle was struck by the fear in their eyes. For the very first time the passengers began to realise the gravity of the situation. Almost immediately an officer arrived and quietly asked the ladies to go to the promenade deck, but as the couples began to step out of the saloon the officer clarified his meaning: 'Women and children will go to the promenade deck. The men will remain where they are.'

The situation had pretty much returned to normal in the smoking room even though the room's occupants had thinned out considerably. A few card games were still moving right along, though, and the players were concentrating on their cards instead of being distracted by events taking place out on deck. When Colonel Gracie came up the stairs to A deck, his arms laden with blankets for the lifeboats, he began looking into doorways in an attempt to locate his two companions. As he glanced into the smoking room he initially thought it was deserted, but then he spotted four men sitting together. Clarence Moore, Major Butt, artist Frank Millet and a fourth gentleman unknown to Gracie were still seated at their card table and seemed oblivious to the happenings on the deck outside, preferring to sit alone in the room where they had spent many enjoy-able hours during the past few evenings. Howard Case and the three sharps were apparently still seated in the room as well.

Presently, the smoking room steward stepped outside onto the open deck for a few moments and then returned to the smoking room to make a somewhat disquieting announcement: 'Gentlemen, the accident looks serious. They are lowering away the boats for women and children.'

The three sharps must have looked at each other uncertainly for a moment but again picked up their hands and prepared to con-tinue their game. The steward, however, in walking past their table, looked meaningfully at the three grifters and said quietly, 'You had better get on deck.'

Upon hearing this, the three sharps rose without even taking time to count up their cheques and settle their accounts (winnings that reportedly amounted to $1,500). Howard Case told Harry Homer he did not think the excitement would amount to anything, but the con men decided to go out on deck to see for themselves. As they were leaving the smoking room the gamblers observed another card game in progress (possibly an eight-handed poker game). As these players looked up and saw the three sharps making a hasty exit, they stopped their play and began to count up their cheques even though Brereton, Romaine and Homer felt the players were making a mistake in delaying their departure. 'We rushed up on deck,' one of the sharps (probably Brereton) remembered later. 'We did not see the fourth man of our game again, and what became of the poor devil I do not know.'

Steward Fred Ray was on his way to the boat deck to take his sta-tion at lifeboat no. 9 and, as he passed the smoking room, he noticed a number of people coming out, among them Clarence Moore. In common with the other men, Moore apparently wanted to size up the situation for himself and joined the exodus from the smoking room. It was about 12.25 a.m.

As they stepped outside onto the open deck, one of the con men was struck by the beauty of the heavens. It was cold but 'the night was clear', he later recalled. 'More stars than I have ever seen lighted the sky.' Many passengers were already on deck, most of them wearing bulky white lifebelts that seemed completely out of place considering the normality of the scene. Nothing was visibly wrong with the vessel and the lights were all burning brightly, the only extraordinary occurrence being a deafening roar from overhead as steam was vented from the safety valves atop the ship's funnels.

The *Titanic* seemed to be the very essence of safety and security but, in spite of this, the officers had swung out a couple of the starboard lifeboats and lowered them level with the boat deck. Crewmen were having considerable difficulty inducing people to step into them, though, because the boats were suspended over the water so that if a mishap occurred it would mean a 60ft drop to the icy blackness of the ocean below. Charles Romaine said later, 'None wanted to leave the *Titanic*. They believed she was perfectly safe … It was my opinion the officers were making a mountain out of a molehill, and I had no intention of getting into any of the boats.' Harry Homer agreed, saying, 'We are safer here than on Broadway', so the three sharps decided to sit back and await developments. Howard Case felt the same way and joked with Fred Seward about the fears that were beginning to be shown by some of the ladies. He even refused to put on a lifebelt.

The gamblers watched the first boat as the officers attempted to fill it with passengers. After fifteen or twenty minutes they managed to partially fill it with women and children and also with men who wished to accompany their wives. Nobody else seemed willing to go, so the boat was lowered away. The same reluctance to leave the ship was evident at the next couple of lifeboats. If men wished to enter the boats they were allowed to do so, since there were not enough women to fill the vacant seats.

Shortly before 1 a.m. Edith Graham approached Howard Case as he stood beside lifeboat no. 3. She was unsure if she should get into a boat or remain on the ship, but Case recommended that she and her daughter enter the lifeboat. When asked what he intended to do, Case replied, 'Oh, I'll take a chance and stay here.' As her boat was lowered away, Edith Graham watched as Howard Case nonchalantly lit a cigarette and waved goodbye to her.

Mr and Mrs Clark had also come on deck, and they watched as men and women entered the first boats and were lowered away. People were alert but unafraid.

While watching the loading of the first lifeboats, one of the gamblers saw the need to have reliable information about the ship's true condition. He had noticed how easy it was for men to enter the first boats and, as he said later, 'We rightly figured it would be a wise move to be in a lifeboat if anything should happen to the *Titanic* ... If she was not injured she would not sail away and leave us in mid-ocean.' Before risking a midnight ride in a small boat, though, the gambler wished to know if it was absolutely necessary, so he began to look around the deck for crew members who were in a position to know how serious the trouble really was.

The gambler's brief indecision took the option of entering a lifeboat out of his own hands, because the situation at the davits had slowly begun to change. An officer approached the Clarks and explained the necessity for the women and children to leave the ship. He said the men would remain behind and would be taken care of later but that it was imperative for the women to leave as soon as possible. Many women did not look favourably on this idea, and when Henry Harris told his wife that he intended to put her in a lifeboat she replied firmly, 'I will wait and go with you.'

The gamblers were unable to obtain satisfactory information about the damage to the *Titanic*, but now they noticed the ship was down slightly at the head and, of greater significance, that men were now forbidden to enter the lifeboats. Periodically, a distress rocket would streak from the bridge area up into the night sky and detonate in a brilliant shower of stars. A faint sense of foreboding must have arisen in the back of their minds because the sharps decided to go below decks to question the firemen and stokers. One of the gamblers correctly reasoned, 'They would surely know what was up with the ship.' Finding a companionway, the three grifters headed down towards the orlop deck with the intention of interrogating crewmen about the ship's true condition.

It might have been during their trip below decks that one of the three encountered young Madeleine Mellinger and her mother as they ascended the staircase towards the boat deck. Madeleine recalled:

> The elevator was *not* running, but I remember for we had to walk up all those stairs. On the way up we met a *beautiful* man who had made friends with me. He was a professional gambler. He told mother he had had a big night, and I wondered what he [meant] until she told me what he was. I thought he was grand (me 13 years old).

The three gamblers continued down towards the lower decks and, before long, they encountered members of the 'black gang' and learned the frightening truth: the *Titanic* had received her death wound and had about an hour to live. George Brereton, Charles Romaine and Harry Homer must have looked at each other in stunned silence. They were used to taking a gambler's chance of being caught while fleecing a lamb, but the stakes had suddenly been raised. Now they were playing in earnest, and their lives would be forfeit if they lost.

The three men turned and clattered up the metal stairways towards the boat deck, but by the time they arrived there the lifeboat situation had got worse. Around each of the lifeboats a crowd had collected, enough people to fill three times the number of boats available. Stationed between the passengers and the boats stood the ship's officers, whose terse commands could be clearly heard by the three grifters: 'Get back, you men! Women and children first!'

According to one of the sharps, 'There seemed to be no escape. There was no chance to get into the lifeboats from the upper decks where they were launched.' The gamblers consulted each other as to their best course of action, but, since fruitful ideas were not forth-coming, the three men again decided to go below and ask the crew how they could save themselves. This time the grifters met some of the engine crew coming up the stairs, and these crewmen brought grim news: the sea was not to be denied. The flooded compartments forward were pulling the *Titanic* down by the head, and the deck was steadily increasing its slant as the water rose. There was nothing anyone could do to save the ship but, as long as the pumps worked and the lights held out, the inevitable could be delayed – nothing more.

'… there seemed to be no escape.'

'Fate Deals a Hand.'

Fear gripped the three gamblers as they again rushed up towards the boat deck but, by the time they arrived, the alarm of the passengers there had increased. Heartbreaking scenes were being enacted as families were parted, women bidding uncertain farewells to their menfolk who must remain behind. Even so, a few people were islands of calm in the midst of the excitement and, in referring to these people, one of the gamblers described:

Sights that made us feel brave. The notable case was that of Mr and Mrs Straus. I doubt if either of them feared the inevitable. Their heroism few of us understand, but it tended to calm us. It gave us fortitude.

92

Romaine later recalled Colonel Astor, Major Butt and Mr and Mrs Straus walking among the crowded groups of passengers trying to calm the growing alarm. Homer reported seeing the Strauses standing next to a lifeboat (apparently no. 8), and Ida Straus's maid Ellen Bird was seated in the boat while several passengers were attempting to force Mr Straus to get into it with his wife. An officer made them stop, since Mr Straus was unwilling to leave the ship before the other men. Mrs Straus clung to her husband, refusing to be parted from him, so boat no. 8 was lowered away at about 1 a.m. while the Strauses stood together on the deck. Then, according to Homer, 'They strolled away together aft, arm in arm. That was the last we saw of them, and I suppose the last the world will ever know of them. They were game.'

Romaine overheard someone say that the *Titanic*'s older sister, the *Olympic*, had been contacted by wireless and would arrive in about thirty-six hours. Even so, the three sharps knew they were being backed into a tight corner. One of the gamblers later said, 'We saw a man pulled out of a lifeboat for the third time. The officer threatened to shoot if he got in again.' Shortly after this, the card men heard shots coming from another part of the ship, probably fired by Fifth Officer Lowe as he was being lowered away in boat no. 14. Lowe had discharged his revolver along the ship's side in order to prevent an avalanche of passengers from leaping into the boat as it passed the lower decks. The time was 1.25 a.m.

May Futrelle was another woman who did not wish to leave her husband. Twice Jacques Futrelle had escorted her to a lifeboat, and twice she returned to her husband's side. Eventually, Mr Futrelle made his wife realise she was hampering his chances to save himself; alone he might be able to swim to a lifeboat, but he could not save himself if she went into the water too. Finally, Mr Futrelle put his wife into boat no. 9 with the whispered plea, 'Remember the children', and the boat was lowered away at around 1.30 a.m.

The first-class smoking room was empty now with the exception of one person. Thomas Andrews, the man who had supervised the building of the *Titanic*, was standing there alone, arms folded, his lifebelt lying on a nearby table. An assistant steward passing through the room saw him there and addressed him, 'Aren't you going to have a try for it, Mr Andrews?' Thomas Andrews was lost in thought, did not move or answer, gave no sign that he had heard. The steward hurried on, leaving him there alone.

One can only wonder what Andrews's thoughts might have been as he stood alone in the smoking room. His brand-new ship, a labour of love, was about to founder, and almost 1,500 people were still on board her. Andrews must have known what was about to happen and must have been heartbroken.

In desperation the three gamblers conferred with each other, trying to devise a plan whereby they could escape the dying liner. Looking over a railing, they watched one of the earlier lifeboats being lowered down towards the water, swinging slowly in and out from the *Titanic*'s side. Seeing this, George Brereton had an inspiration.

'Boys,' he said, 'I'm going to get a boat.' With that, Brereton turned and hurried towards the companionway that led below, and Romaine and Homer were right behind him.

The three men emerged on the promenade deck and hurried to the rail where another lifeboat was slowly descending from above, drawing steadily nearer and nearer to the gamblers. Finally, the boat was level with the railing, suspended about 3ft out from the side of the ship. 'There were some women in it,' one of the gamblers (probably Brereton) remembered, 'but the occupants were mostly coal heavers.' At that point he made his move.

'I jumped up on the rail, and as it was lowered I sprang in,' Brereton related later. 'There wasn't anybody to tell me to get out, and I doubt very much that I would have paid much attention to such an order.' Romaine and Homer were close behind, half-jumping and half-diving for the boat. One of the gamblers later recalled, 'It was our only chance and we took it. Seven stokers also jumped with us. That is the truth. I don't know whether it was manly or not, but we escaped.'

The lifeboat continued its jerky descent towards the water and settled at last into the sea. The falls were then disconnected, and the boat slowly began to pull away from the *Titanic*'s side. (One gambler said the lifeboat in question was the 'third boat', and in one interview 'George Brayton' claimed he swam away from the *Titanic* and was picked up by Third Officer Pitman in boat no. 5. However, the present writer believes the gamblers probably left the ship in boat no. 15 since 'H. Haven' later specified this boat as being the one he 'reluctantly entered'. Boat no. 15 left the ship at around 1.40 a.m.)

'… it was our only chance and we took it.'

The people who looked back at the ship as their lifeboats pulled away were startled by what they saw. The *Titanic* was well down at the bow, the brightly lit rows of portholes disappearing into the sea as she settled. It was this sight that brought home to many people the shocking realisation that the *Titanic* was truly sinking. May Futrelle tried to close her eyes and shut out the scene but could not. It held a horrible fascination for her. She thought of her husband still on board the big liner and began to pray.

Mr and Mrs Clark were still on board the ship as well. They had stood together for more than an hour watching the boats leaving the ship, but eventually there was only one full-sized lifeboat remaining to be launched from the forward davits. Walter Clark still seemed unconcerned about the ship's safety, but finally decided to follow the officer's instructions and put his wife into boat no. 4. Virginia Clark later recalled that, from the way her husband bade her goodbye, she knew he fully expected to join her later. Colonel John Jacob Astor placed his young bride in boat no. 4 as well and then stepped back and joined Mr Clark in assisting other ladies into the boat. It is ironic to think that Walter Clark and John Jacob Astor should spend their final hour in each other's company, since Clark had been targeted as a potential victim of the three gamblers and Astor had been named as the prime target of 'Doc' Owen's confidence game. The two men had each received a reprieve from the proposed stings, but at a terrible price.

Boat no. 4 was lowered away, but the water was no longer 60ft below the boat deck. After descending only 20ft the lifeboat reached the surface of the sea, and passengers watched as water poured into the open portholes of the *Titanic*'s upper decks. It was 1.50 a.m.

The last of the full-sized boats was away, which left only the four collapsible Engelhardt boats, A, B, C and D. Collapsible D was wrestled to the davits that had been used to lower boat no. 2, and

Colonel Astor approached Henry Harris and his wife, Renée, who were standing nearby. 'Harris, put your wife in the next boat. We'll make for the rafts. There isn't much time to be lost.'

Despite her broken arm, Renée Harris insisted on remaining with her husband. The couple then walked through the bridge area, where they encountered Captain Edward Smith, Major Archibald Butt and Dr William O'Loughlin. The captain appeared dumbfounded when he saw that Mrs Harris was still on board.

'My God, woman,' he cried. 'Why aren't you in a lifeboat?'

Renée Harris repeated her mantra that she would not leave her husband, and Dr O'Loughlin chuckled, 'Isn't she a brick?'

'She's a little fool,' Captain Smith replied. 'She's handicapping her husband's chances to save himself.'

Upon being assured that there were plenty of rafts in the stern for the men, Renée Harris finally allowed her husband to lift her into collapsible D. At 2.05 a.m., as the boat began its 10ft descent to the water, she saw her husband standing next to Colonel Astor and Jacques Futrelle. Harris and Futrelle had both seen their wives to safety, and the crooked poker game of the day before was very far from their minds.

Howard Case was standing quietly at the railing a bit further aft when Algernon Barkworth approached him and asked if he intended to take his chances and swim from the liner's side.

'My dear fellow,' Case replied, 'I wouldn't think of quitting the ship. Why, she'll swim for a week.' As Case said this he calmly took out a cigarette and lit it, but this was not very reassuring to Barkworth due to the fact that the *Titanic*'s bow had just made an ominous dip downward. Climbing up on the railing, Barkworth hesitated for a moment and then jumped feet first into the water.

Howard Case had enjoyed his last game of bridge whist, and Algernon Barkworth was the last person to see him alive on board the *Titanic*. It was 2.10 a.m. The end was very near.

From the lifeboats, people watched the ship with fascination and dread. The forecastle deck was underwater now, and the great screws aft had risen clear of the sea. The *Titanic* was still brightly lit, but one by one the forward portholes winked out as they dipped beneath the surface. The slope of the deck increased. Hundreds of people could be seen lining the rails, moving aft, leaping into the sea. The ship's band was still playing, and people listened in wonder as the strains of the hymn 'Nearer, My God, to Thee' floated out across the clear night. The *Titanic*'s bridge began to submerge and, as it went under, a great wave surged over the boat deck sweeping away everyone in its path. The wire stays supporting the ship's forward funnel gave way and, with a shower of sparks, it toppled forward into the midst of a group of struggling swimmers. The great stern rose relentlessly, majestically into the sky until it eventually reached an angle approaching 30 degrees.

Suddenly, darkness. The lights had finally failed, but those closest to the *Titanic* could still see her, a black silhouette against the starry heavens. And everyone could hear her. Deep, booming reports rose from the depths of the ship and rumbled across the water as the vessel's stern tore itself away from the bow section and settled back onto the ocean's surface as if it were going to float on its own. But this lasted for only a few moments. Then, like a mammoth spectre, the stern gradually began rearing itself out of the water again, higher, steeper, until to some survivors it appeared to tower almost vertically into the sky. For a few moments the ship hung there in silence, suspended between life and death, beckoning to the silent stars. Then, very slowly, the *Titanic* began to lose her buoyancy and finally gave up her fight for life. She began to move downwards, gradually picked up speed and slid gracefully beneath the surface of the sea. It was 2.20 a.m.

George Brereton watched in awe as the great liner went down. 'We saw the afterdeck crowded with men,' he later recalled. 'We saw

'Oh, what a night that was.'

the fateful plunge of the giant steamer. We saw the men on the after-deck go overboard like frogs jumping from a bank. And then! Oh, what a night that was!'

The people in the lifeboats stared silently at the place where the *Titanic* had just disappeared, but then, steadily increasing in volume, a terrible sound came to them from out of the darkness. Almost 1,500 human beings were struggling for their lives in the freezing water, and their wild, hopeless, heart-shaking cries of agony filled the night. The men and women in the boats were stricken with horror at the sound, for they realised that friends and loved ones were among the teeming mass of humanity dying there in the water.

The three gamblers sat in their lifeboat and listened to the terrible shrieks and moans of the dying, and Brereton was badly shaken by the experience. Later he recalled:

Oh, the wails and the mourning, the cries and the gurgling shouts I heard while doubled up in the bottom of that boat. How long they lasted! There was room for many more in our boat … If I could only have answered a call. A cheering 'halloa' or a false reply that we were coming. Nothing of the kind. We sat, mute and dumb, until the cries, like an easing pain, ceased.

One of the gamblers later claimed that 'a man swam up to the boat with a child. Somebody said it was Captain Smith. The child was taken aboard and the man swam back to the *Titanic*.' Brereton also claimed that his boat picked up six people from the sea. The truth of these claims is doubtful, but the fact remains that George Brereton, Charles Romaine and Harry Homer had managed to save themselves while many hundreds of people were dying around them. By the time the cries of the swimmers finally ceased, John Jacob Astor, Henry Harris, Jacques Futrelle, Howard Case and Walter Clark had all perished, along with 1,491 other passengers and crewmen of the 'unsinkable' *Titanic*.

While his lifeboat floated idly on the smooth surface of the sea, Romaine suddenly recalled that the *Olympic* was thirty-six hours away. He felt that 'if the sea remained calm, and we had food and water, that we could all last it out'. He asked several dining room stewards whether the lifeboat contained any provisions, but they did not know. According to Romaine, nobody knew how to properly pull an oar, so 'I had to take charge and show them how to row together'.

Our next glimpse of the gamblers comes from a brief mention of them in a story by Thomas Logan in the *Philadelphia Inquirer*. Logan's source of information is unknown, but – in light of later events on the *Carpathia* – it has an authentic ring to it.

Logan stated that the gamblers' only concern during the sinking had been to get into a lifeboat. Two of them succeeded in doing so, after which they resumed their usual suave, polite manner and even refused to allow the women in their boat to do any rowing. In order to shore up the flagging spirits of the widows in the boat, the sharps waxed eloquent about the mysterious ways the Almighty uses in carrying out His will and pointed out that good always comes from evil.

'Who knows?' said one gambler. 'It may be that everybody on board will be saved.'

'Our duty is to the living,' said the other. 'You women owe it to your relatives and friends not to allow this thing to wreck your reason or undermine your health.'

For the most part, the occupants of the lifeboats were silent, weighed down by the tragic events that had just transpired. Some women wept quietly, and many people were poorly dressed and began to suffer intensely from the piercing chill of the night.

'Cold!' Brereton remembered. 'Oh, it was cold! Men almost froze in the boats and the women only kept alive by taking their "tricks" at the oars with the men.'

And so the night passed ...

5

THE *CARPATHIA*, NEW YORK AND AFTERWARDS

At about 4 a.m. the eastern sky began to brighten faintly, and the survivors in the lifeboats gradually became aware of their immediate surroundings.

'It was a radiant dawn,' May Futrelle remembered. 'The rising sun cast a pink reflection on the horizon. There was a long, dead swell on the sea.'

Renée Harris observed the sunrise from her own vantage point in collapsible D. 'I looked around and could see for the first time what seemed like mountains of ice surrounding us,' she recalled. 'Dotted all over the water were thousands of spots of ice, broken bits from the berg that the *Titanic* had struck.'

But more importantly, a ship was visible in the distance. The *Carpathia* had come, completing her dash through the night to aid the stricken *Titanic*. With renewed hope, the lifeboats began to pull towards the Cunarder and, one by one, they moved up to the *Carpathia*'s cliff-like side and were secured there while preparations were made to take the survivors on board. With ropes tied securely around their waists, some of the women climbed rope ladders to the open cargo doors in the ship's side, while others sat in a rope swing and were hoisted aboard. The men climbed unaided, and children made the ascent in mail bags hauled up by willing hands.

Renée Harris made the ascent seated in a rope swing and was carried into a large room crowded with men and women. After sitting there for several hours she was approached by a steward, who discovered she was a first-class passenger and apologised for putting her with the steerage passengers. With a steward supporting either arm, she was escorted from the room.

As Renée was assisted along the deck, another *Titanic* survivor approached her – the same man her husband had suspected of being a professional gambler. She was stunned and later recalled, 'I wanted to shriek, "YOU were saved, and my beloved has been taken away from me!"' So great was her grief and rage that she could not say a word, but the gambler spoke to her in his suave manner and said, 'Do not grieve. It is God's will.' Upon hearing those words Renée unleashed her pent-up fury upon the hapless sharp and, for the next four days, until the *Carpathia* reached New York, the gambler immediately left the vicinity whenever the widow of Henry Harris approached.

'YOU were saved, and my beloved has been taken away from me!'

May Futrelle was also taken on board the *Carpathia*, but the loss of her husband had drained her of all feeling, depriving her of the emotional release that tears might bring. It was ironic, therefore, that this same gambler was one of the first men she saw on board the rescue ship, and she saw that he wore the same cynical smile she had seen on his face the night he was pointed out to her on the *Titanic*. It was a cruel twist of fate that this sharp was also assigned a seat across from her at the dining room table.

'It was horrible to hear him talk,' May Futrelle remembered. Without regard for the feelings of the *Titanic*'s widows, the sharp made the comment that it was every man for himself after the *Titanic* was struck, adding that there must really be something to the law of the 'survival of the fittest'. She felt it was better that her husband had died like a man instead of surviving and being compared to this professional gambler.

George Brereton, Charles Romaine and Harry Homer were safe on board the rescue ship, but all around them were scenes of anguish. According to Homer, 'Aboard the *Carpathia* there was much of discomfort and of horror. The French women whose husbands were lost were uncontrollable, and nearly all the steerage women rescued had been bereaved.' He described how Margaret Brown of Denver organised a group of volunteer nurses and helpers to try to alleviate some of the suffering on board. Many survivors had come aboard without any money or proper clothing and, according to a *Carpathia* passenger, 'a relief committee was formed and our passengers contributed enough for their immediate needs'.

The accuracy of the information in the following paragraph is unknown, because it comes from a *very* unreliable newspaper interview the gamblers granted. It is just possible, though, that it might contain a few kernels of truth.

According to the three sharps, after boarding the *Carpathia* they went to the ship's barber shop and bought themselves sweaters and caps before going back on deck and mingling with other passengers. Presently, they suggested that a relief fund be initiated to assist in clothing and outfitting those survivors who had nothing, and, taking off their caps, they put in the bills and coins they had in their pockets and proceeded to tour the ship on their 'mission of mercy'. Eventually, two of the sharps arrived at the cabin of the ship's surgeon that had a sign on the door reading 'Don't knock', but they went in anyway. Inside the cabin they found survivor J. Bruce Ismay, chairman of the White Star Line. (If this story is true, the two gamblers must have been Homer and Brereton, since Romaine said he did not know Ismay by sight and did not know if he had ever seen him.) When the two gamblers told Ismay about their relief fund, he replied, 'Why, the White Star Company will care for all these people when they land in New York. Don't worry yourselves about them.' One of the sharps persisted, pointing out that many survivors were without clothing and money, but Ismay repeated, 'They'll get all that when they get to New York. Don't worry me further.' With that, Ismay waved the two grifters out of the cabin, so they continued their rounds and eventually collected $700 in cash and $9,300 in signatures and cheques. The sharps then bought out the ship's barber and distributed sweaters, shoes and stockings to the needy survivors.

According to survivor Fred Seward, the *Carpathia*'s barber freely distributed travellers' supplies to those *Titanic* survivors who had no money. Nothing was said about mass purchases by the relief committee, so if there is any truth to the gamblers' account of their personal relief fund, this writer strongly suspects they had a respectable sum of money left over after completing their purchases from the *Carpathia*'s barber. (It seems unlikely that a sudden moral conversion would prevent the three men from achieving one final 'sting' when the opportunity presented itself – and that is assuming they did not keep the entire relief fund as one of their spoils of war.)

Homer told of seeing the widow of John Jacob Astor on the *Carpathia* when she emerged briefly from her cabin. Madeleine Astor did not look like a bride who had recently been honeymooning all over Europe with her new husband. 'Her eyes looked old and tired,' Homer observed, 'and there was a wondering look in them, as if she did not quite comprehend.'

Another incident impressed Homer as being a 'tragedy within a tragedy'. Four bodies were taken aboard the *Carpathia* before the *Titanic*'s lifeboats were hoisted on deck and, late on the afternoon of 15 April, the bodies were consigned to the deep after a brief religious service. Homer felt the burials should have taken place after dark and later remarked, 'Why the officers of the rescue ship chose to add to the misery of the voyage by committing the bodies to the deep when the decks were filled with men and women already horror-stricken, is beyond me.'

With this sad task completed, the *Carpathia* turned her bows back towards New York and wirelessed the *Olympic* and other ships about the *Titanic*'s fate, and the grim news was relayed ashore to a shocked world. On 16 April, the *Carpathia*'s Marconi operator began sending out a list of survivors for retransmission to a shore station and, when asked for their names, George Brereton and Charles Romaine gave the purser their aliases of 'George Brayton' and 'C. Rolmane'. Harry Homer, on the other hand, was apparently listed twice on the roster, once as 'H. Haven' and once as 'Henry Homer', because each name appears in several published lists of survivors.

Meanwhile, in Indianapolis, Indiana, Mrs Louise Logsdon was going about her normal routine when she was told of the *Titanic* disaster. Her brother, Harry Haven Homer, had been abroad for the past two months and had last written to her from Cairo, but Mrs Logsdon somehow felt positive he had booked his passage home on the *Titanic*. So certain was she that she told her friends and neighbours of her conviction and immediately began buying every newspaper she could find. In scanning the lists of passengers, Mrs Logsdon may have seen the name 'H. Haven', a name very similar to that of her brother. She kept looking, though, and eventually she was rewarded by finding a list of survivors containing the name 'Henry Homer'. The conflicting reports, coupled with the presence and absence of Homer's name on various lists, kept Mrs Logsdon in a state of anxiety, and she had no way of knowing whether her brother was safe or not. Another brother, W.H. Homer of New Albany, had seen the name 'Henry Homer' on the survivor roster but was not certain if this man was his brother, since the latter usually wrote his name as 'Harry' Homer. And so, for the time being, his relatives were left in a state of uncertainty regarding his fate.

Nor were they the only ones, because the entire gambling fraternity in New York was alive with rumours and speculation about which con men had succeeded in booking passage on the *Titanic*.

Al McPherson, the grifter who had decided to skip *Titanic*'s maiden voyage because of seasickness, told a New York reporter he had heard that 'Doc' Owen, 'Jimmie' Bell and Ernest 'Peaches' Jeffery had all been on board the doomed vessel. McPherson noticed that *Titanic*'s second-class passenger list contained the names 'Ernest and Clifford Jeffereys' and, since Ernest 'Peaches' Jeffery did not have a brother named Clifford, McPherson opined that 'Jimmie' Bell had sailed using that name as his alias. (In truth, brothers Ernest and Clifford Jeffereys were travelling with their sister Lillian Renouf, and both men were lost in the sinking.)

McPherson told the reporter that a cable from England received on the night of 17 April claimed that 'Peaches' and 'Jack Day' had both failed to board the *Titanic* and were still in England; McPherson did not believe this report, though, since he felt that *Titanic*'s maiden voyage 'pickings' would have been too tempting for the two men to ignore.

Unknown to McPherson, on the afternoon of 17 April a wireless message was allegedly received from two of the surviving sharps who were now on the *Carpathia*. The men supposedly signed themselves 'George Homer' and 'Ralph Bradley', the message allegedly being sent to friends in New York. The message stated that the two men were safe on the *Carpathia* but that Tom McAuliffe, William Dey and 'Peaches' Van Camp had gone down with the *Titanic*. Later that evening, another Marconigram from Homer and 'Bradley' was allegedly received by 'a well-known New York sporting man' stating that 'Buffalo' Murphy and James Gordon were apparently not on board the *Carpathia* either and that they, too, must have perished.

In truth, only two of the *Titanic*'s surviving sharps attempted to send Marconigrams while the *Carpathia* was at sea, but only one of them was successful in doing so. On 17 April, Harry Homer sent a wireless to his wife at the Empire Hotel at 63rd and Broadway saying, 'Mother Coming safe. Telephone Grace. Harry'. It is uncertain if

'Mother' might have been Homer's pet name for his wife, but 'Grace' was almost certainly a reference to George Brereton's fiancée Grace. (If so, it appears that the Homers and the Breretons were friends in a social sense in addition to the gambling relationship that existed between the two men.)

It is a good thing that Homer asked his wife to telephone George Brereton's wife, because Brereton's own Marconigram was addressed to 'Bell' at 550 West 170th in New York City, the message itself reading simply, 'Arriving *Carpathia* meet Boat' and signed, 'Brayton'. Unfortunately, Brereton's wireless message was never transmitted and never reached its intended recipient, because *Carpathia*'s wireless operator was overloaded with messages submitted to him by other survivors.

The New York underworld continued to hum with rumours about the sharps who had supposedly perished on the *Titanic*. Many con men were aware that several sharps had been saved and half a dozen supposedly lost, but they were uncertain just who these men were. Names contained in the alleged wireless messages from the *Carpathia* became jumbled with those of men only rumoured to be on board the *Titanic* and, in that way, a large number of con men were reported to have perished in the disaster. The list was a good blend of rumour, names, nicknames and aliases, and a list of these men follows. (None of them were on board the *Titanic*.)

(1) 'Buffalo' Murphy.

(2) 'Old Man' Jordan. In 1912 James Jordan was thought to be about 80 years old and was said to have been cheating for seventy-five of those years. He had played all the con games, from the green goods game to selling gold bricks. Jordan was said to be financially secure in France but that he nevertheless decided to cash in on the *Titanic*'s maiden voyage.

(3) Jim Kitchener. Originally came from the Midwest and was an outstanding card mechanic. He had 'followed the sea' for the past ten years.

(4) 'Tricky' Silverton. An alias of Harry Silberberg, who we discussed earlier in this book.

(5) 'One-arm Mac'. A nickname for Tom McAuliffe, the supposed leader of the *Titanic* sharps, who was also discussed earlier.

(6) Ernest 'Peaches' Jeffery. Also known as 'Peaches Van Camp'.

(7) 'Jack Day'. Nickname of William Dey.

(8) 'Jimmie' Bell. According to Al McPherson, 'He was a good fellow and staked many a man who was down and out on the "Great White Way".'

(9) 'Doc' Owen. Real name Joseph Cohn. Turned up alive in London.

(10) 'Black Mike'. Real name unknown. An old-time con man, his specialty was the 'wire game' in which a victim was led to believe that Mike's confederate was receiving advance information on horse-racing results.

(11) James Gordon.

(12) 'Doctor Beagle'. Real name unknown. An excellent linguist, which he put to good use in his con games. 'Doc' had two ugly scars, one on his cheek and one on his forehead, and he always kept his hair clear of the latter one so that it was always visible. He told his victims he received his scars in duels at the University of Heidelberg. This was probably not true, but Doc was a good student of human nature and knew that this story about his exotic past would assist him in getting close to a potential victim.

Before the *Carpathia*'s arrival in New York brought an end to the speculation, all of the above con men were rumoured to have gone down with the *Titanic*. Characteristically, New York's gambling fraternity showed no sympathy for those sharps who supposedly perished, and one gambler made those callous sentiments clear in an interview he granted on 18 April:

Say, seventy or eighty men were saved, weren't they? Take it from me, if those fellows couldn't get in among that many men, they don't deserve any sympathy. If they've had no more enterprise than to stay there and drown it's a wonder how they ever made a living.

The general consensus of opinion was that the surviving sharps might have disguised themselves as women or sailors in order to take a place in one of the lifeboats.

The *Carpathia* continued on her way towards New York and, at one point, Spencer Silverthorne fell into conversation with an acquaintance, 'Mr. Romaine of Louisville, Kentucky'. Charles Romaine told Silverthorne that on the night of the collision he and his fellow bridge players had been playing for 5 cents a point ('a pretty stiff game' in Silverthorne's opinion) and that their game had continued for approximately ten minutes after the collision before they decided to call a halt and settle their accounts. Romaine claimed he owed his opponents around $76 when the game ended, but he had

Charles Stengel.

not had time to go down to his stateroom and retrieve the $1,200 he had hidden in the pocket of a dress shirt he had locked inside his steamer trunk. The end result was that Romaine was nearly broke on board the rescue ship and, in sharing this information, it might well have been the gambler's intention to mulct a few dollars from Spencer Silverthorne or possibly even set him up as the prospective victim for a future con job.

George Brereton was apparently having similar ideas while *Carpathia* continued onward towards New York, because on 17 April survivor Charles Stengel was walking along the deck when he saw a man who looked so dejected that Stengel felt moved to talk with him and find out what the trouble was. 'Mr. Stengel, I have lost everything,' replied 'George Brayton'. Although surprised that the stranger knew his name, Stengel did not give the matter much thought as 'Brayton' explained that he had lost all his money in the sinking and did not know how he was going to get home to Los Angeles. Stengel, a Newark leather manufacturer, advised 'Brayton' to ask the White Star Line for the money, and the gambler claimed he had not thought of that option and thanked Stengel for his suggestion. Mr Stengel kindly assured 'George Brayton' that he would advance him the money himself if the White Star Line proved reluctant to help.

This meeting between Charles Stengel and George Brereton on the *Carpathia* was just the opening gambit of a con game that Brereton intended to pull on Stengel after the rescue ship reached New York.

The *Carpathia* finally drew near the American coast after encountering ice, thunderstorms and fog while steaming towards New York. Her eventful journey drew to a close on the night of 18 April when she entered New York Harbor and was immediately surrounded by tugs bearing an army of newspaper reporters. Captain Rostron's reticence in transmitting information ashore concerning the disaster had intensified the world's thirst for news and, as the tugs moved along next to the *Carpathia*, the reporters shouted questions to the people lining her rail. One enterprising reporter from the *New York American* even managed to leap from his tugboat onto the *Carpathia* through an open cargo door in the ship's side. This reporter was able to obtain brief interviews with a couple of survivors before a ship's officer seized him and hauled him unceremoniously onto the upper deck, where he was able to speak with two more survivors, who gave their names as 'H.H. Haven' and 'George A. Brayton'.

'Haven' (Harry Homer) did most of the talking and told the reporter that he and 'Brayton' (George Brereton) had been playing pinochle at the time of the collision. He went on to describe the general behaviour of the *Titanic's* passengers during the evacuation, his account being very believable, but on a closing note, 'Haven' claimed that Jacques Futrelle had been separated from his wife at the point of an officer's revolver. This fabricated addition to the story

Harry Homer grants his first interview.

was just the first of many falsehoods that were invented by the three gamblers in telling reporters about their *Titanic* experiences. (In the present case, one cannot help but wonder if Homer might have been revenging himself on May Futrelle for possibly saying something uncomplimentary about him while they were seated across the table from each other in the *Carpathia*'s dining room.)

After obtaining his interview with two of the surviving sharps, the *New York American* reporter stood with them on deck as the *Carpathia* neared the Cunard pier. Gazing ashore, they beheld thousands of people crowding the waterfront awaiting their arrival.

The tension on shore was almost unbearable, and friends and relatives of the *Titanic*'s passengers were anxiously looking forward to being reunited with their loved ones. Published lists of survivor names were contradictory, though, and many people did not know whether their loved ones were among the living or the dead. They waited, hoping against hope, as the *Carpathia* docked and the gangplank was extended to her side.

Seven hundred and twelve *Titanic* survivors made their way from the *Carpathia* down onto the pier, their relatives offering up prayers of thanksgiving for their safety. But the relatives of 1,496 victims waited in vain for the faces of their loved ones to appear at the railing.

George Brereton, Charles Romaine and Harry Homer were met at the pier by their New York friends and, by the next day, it was common knowledge throughout the underworld that three surviving sharps had been seen to walk down the *Carpathia*'s gangplank. The card men told their friends they had been playing bridge when the ship struck and that they managed to get into one of the last lifeboats to leave the ship.

Romaine left the *Carpathia* in the same evening suit he had been wearing when he left the *Titanic*. The gambler expected to be met on the pier by his wife but, when she did not appear, the great nervous strain he had been under began to show its effects and he began to lose control of his emotions. Romaine apologised to a reporter, explaining, 'You might think this is weakness, but we have gone through a good deal.' In his printed interview with Romaine, the reporter mentioned to his readers that Mrs Romaine joined her husband a little later.

All three gamblers must have encountered reporters on the pier, because the morning of 19 April saw several of their stories published in the newspapers. Romaine was the only one to give reporters his true name; Brereton identified himself as both 'George Brayton' and 'George Braden' of Los Angeles, while Harry Homer gave his first interviews as 'H. Haven' of Indianapolis and as 'H.H. Haven' of New York.

Taken individually, some of these first gambler interviews were not too far-fetched, with many of their 'facts' seeming to be perfectly believable, but other interviews were filled with the most blatant of falsehoods. The one thing these stories all had in common was that none of them had anything to do with the gamblers' true activities on board the *Titanic*. For instance, 'George Braden' said he had been in his stateroom at the time of the collision, but in another interview 'George Brayton' claimed to have been walking on the *Titanic*'s deck and that he saw the iceberg before the collision. Romaine related several versions of his own story as well, telling one reporter he had just retired for the evening when the ship struck and that he was commanded to row in one of the first lifeboats to leave the ship. His other (and more accurate) versions told how he was seated in the smoking room with Howard Case and Walter Clark (although he did not mention they were playing cards). Romaine even insisted he jumped overboard from the *Titanic* and was picked up by a lifeboat, and similar stories told by 'Brayton' and 'Haven' claimed they had also leaped into the sea and been picked up by lifeboats.

As has been mentioned, some versions of the gamblers' stories might seem believable if they did not contradict each other and if we were unaware of the true identities of these three men. The interviews with 'Brayton' and 'Haven' might possibly contain some factual information about things they actually observed with their own eyes, but, if so, it is impossible to separate the truth from the fiction. For this reason, no interviews with 'Brayton' or 'Haven' have been utilised here in telling the gamblers' story, but several interviews with Romaine appear to be more reliable (up to a point) and have been cautiously referred to in this book.

Within a day or two of arriving in New York, Harry Homer dashed off a quick note to his sister in Indianapolis; the letter was very brief and was not very accurate in relaying the facts, since Homer told Mrs Logsdon he had strapped on a lifebelt and leaped into the sea before the *Titanic* went down and that he had seized a small raft of broken timbers and floated in the icy water for four hours until a lifeboat approached. Homer claimed he was almost unconscious when he was hauled into the lifeboat and that he remembered little that happened before the *Carpathia* took him on board. He told his sister he was suffering from nervous shock and that he intended to take a trip to San Antonio, Texas, for his health before returning to Indianapolis.

Clearly, Louise Logsdon did not know her brother was a professional card sharp, and Harry Homer, just as obviously, was shielding her from that knowledge.

On 20 April, 'George Brayton' telephoned fellow survivor Charles Stengel and told him that, as per Stengel's suggestion on board the *Carpathia*, the White Star Line did indeed provide 'Brayton' with money to travel to Los Angeles. Stengel invited the gambler to dinner at his home that evening and, during the course of the evening's conversation, 'Brayton' spoke of an upcoming New York real estate deal that promised to bring him $65,000; he added that the negotiations for this deal were scheduled to close at about the time his brother-in-law (supposedly an assistant superintendent at Western Union) returned from Mexico. The evening ended cordially, and 'George Brayton' apparently told Charles Stengel that he would stay in touch.

It was also on the evening of 20 April that two of the *Titanic*'s surviving sharps (probably Homer and Brereton) walked into a New York City café owned by a man named Jim Buckley. (In addition to owning the café, Buckley was a well-known Tammany politician and manager of several professional boxers, so it seems probable he was on a first-name basis with many professional gamblers.) The two sharps discussed the disaster with Buckley, who later repeated the story for a reporter. The gamblers said it had been easy for anyone to enter the first four lifeboats and that little persuasion was needed to convince them to get into one. No mention was made of any leap into a lowering lifeboat.

It was at that point that many curious stories about the *Titanic*'s gamblers began to appear in print, each story differing substantially from the others. One of the strangest was a remarkable 'confession' made by one of the surviving sharps. (At least, the gambler in question *claimed* to be a *Titanic* survivor, but whether he was actually just a clever opportunist will never be known.)

The gambler in question approached an unnamed 'New York official' claiming to be the 'lone survivor' of the group of sharps that had sailed on the *Titanic*. In saving himself, the grifter had proved himself to be a coward and so refused to give his name (the official thought) 'lest the scorn of his fellow criminals be more than he can bear'. At any rate, the gambler gave the official a list of more than twenty confidence men who had supposedly perished on the *Titanic*.

The New York official sent a letter to Detective Sergeant Timothy De Roche of Chicago, an acknowledged expert on confidence men. The letter repeated what the lone gambler had said about the twenty con men and told of their 'last moments' as the gambler had supposedly observed them on the *Titanic*.

'Old Man' Jordan was said to be one of the lost sharps who was last seen 'passing a little girl to a frantic mother in a lifeboat'. Harry Silberberg (alias Harry Silverton) was another gambler who was supposedly lost in the disaster. These were the only two sharps De Roche mentioned by name to reporters, but it is almost certain that all the gamblers mentioned earlier in this book were on the list (as well as several who are unknown to us). The 'lone gambler' apparently attributed heroic deaths to all the 'lost' sharps, just as he did for 'Old Man' Jordan.

In speaking about the list of 'lost' gamblers, Detective De Roche expressed a certain regret that these con men had perished. 'All of these men lived lives of luxury when they were in luck and took their medicine gamely when the fates were against them,' he said. 'The police of many cities will rest easier now that they are dead, but for my part I am glad they died like men.'

Whether or not the 'lone surviving gambler' was one of the three surviving sharps is unknown, but it is reasonably certain he had an ulterior motive for making his 'confession'. His compiled list of twenty 'deceased' grifters was a very clever ploy, since, by claiming to have seen these con men with his own eyes on board the *Titanic*, the believability of the 'lone survivor's' story would be strengthened in the eyes of unknowing law enforcement officers. The fact that the gambler refused to reveal his own name virtually assures us that he included it on his list of 'deceased' gamblers. This ploy would have been invaluable in throwing the police off his own trail as well as those of his still-living colleagues since, if the police thought all these sharps were dead, they would of course cease to look for them. The con men could then expect to gain a little breathing room that would enable them to practise their craft without interference from the Pinkerton Agency.

Unfortunately, several friends of Harry Silberberg failed to realise he could benefit from this report of his alleged death on the *Titanic*, because one of his New York colleagues spoke with a reporter on the evening of 21 April and revealed that the report was simply not true. 'I am positive that not more than ten days ago I saw him right here in New York,' the friend declared, 'and naturally I was amused that, on top of all the publicity he had been given, someone had unthinkingly given him a hero role as a finish.'

This man spoke truly for, on the evening of 23 April, Harry Silberberg himself surfaced in Denver, where he dined with friends who reported that he was thoroughly enjoying the reports of his heroic demise. Harry was travelling under an alias but assured his colleagues, 'I am not dead yet.' It turned out that Silberberg left England a week before the *Titanic* sailed. 'Gamblers are superstitious,' he said, 'and I would never think of taking a boat on its maiden voyage.' Silberberg was on his way to the Pacific coast to sail for Honolulu but was now having second thoughts about the advisability of the voyage, since the reported loss of several gambling colleagues on the *Titanic* apparently made him aware of his own mortality.

Meanwhile, back in New York, the three surviving sharps were still in the news. On 23 April 'George Bradley' granted an interview containing several nuggets of truth but, on the whole, it was twisted with contradictions and falsehoods. It was this interview that created the myth of the card game that continued in the *Titanic*'s smoking room until just before the ship foundered. 'Bradley' described the many onlookers who supposedly watched the game until the ship's band began playing 'Nearer, My God, to Thee', at which time everyone went on deck only to discover that all the lifeboats were gone. However, in the very next paragraph 'Bradley' stated (correctly) that they played cards for only forty-five minutes after the collision.

'Bradley' also related that theatrical manager Henry Harris played cards in the smoking room, left to put his wife in a lifeboat and then returned to continue his game. We know this is not true, but it is curious that the gamblers insisted on mentioning Harris in so many of their newspaper interviews. Sometimes they said Harris gallantly kissed his wife goodbye, but at other times they claimed he was driven from a lifeboat at the point of a gun. Perhaps the latter tale was the sharps' way of taking posthumous revenge on Harris, since it was he who suspected one of them of cheating in the shipboard poker game. (Renée Harris, too, had made things very uncomfortable for the sharps while on board the *Carpathia*.) In spite of the fictional elements of his story, 'Bradley' was truthful in telling how he leaped into a lifeboat as it was lowered past him, but he did not mention Harry Homer or Charles Romaine at all.

On the same day that 'George Bradley's' interview appeared in the newspapers, the *New York World* published a small personal item at the bottom of an inside page. *Carpathia* passenger John Badenoch, of R.H. Macy and Co., wanted to communicate with three survivors of the *Titanic* disaster: 'George Drayton' of Los Angeles, 'Mr Haven' of Indianapolis and 'Mr Romaine' of Georgetown, Kentucky. Badenoch gave instructions on how he could be reached but did not reveal the reason he wished to contact the three gamblers. (Perhaps Badenoch wanted to ask them about their newspaper mentions of his employer, Isidor Straus, but one wonders if perhaps he might have played a little bridge whist with the three men on the *Carpathia* and, suspecting that something was not quite right about that game, he now wished to test his suspicions further.)

On 24 April, two additional stories describing the gamblers' rescue were published. The first was fairly truthful, the major discrepancy coming at the point where the three men ran down to the promenade deck in order to leap into a lifeboat. This new account claimed that the three sharps scattered along the deck and waited for different lifeboats to be lowered past them. Homer and Brereton succeeded in jumping into their individual boats, but

Romaine missed his boat, fell into the water and was pulled into another lifeboat.

The unnamed gambler who told this story felt it necessary to justify his own survival when so many other people had died. 'We didn't beat anybody out of a place,' the sharp insisted. 'We were on the level and saved ourselves, and nobody can say we did anything wrong.'

The second 24 April interview was filled with so much melodramatic fiction it would have been laughable if it did not concern a tragedy. Briefly told, the three sharps were playing bridge near an eight-handed poker game, neither game being interrupted by the collision. Later, a steward went outside and returned to tell them of the lowering lifeboats, so the men at the poker game left to see their wives to safety and then returned to their game. The steward, who knew and liked the three sharps, came back and gave them a special warning of the seriousness of the situation, so they went up on deck and 'played the game square' by helping to launch the lifeboats. It was there that Harry Homer saw Mr and Mrs Straus and their maid at a lifeboat, but then one of the gamblers noticed some crewmen working to lower a boat located on the port side. The sharps 'knew' that the port boats were not supposed to be launched until the starboard boats were away, so they rushed over and found twelve stokers trying to lower the boat in secret. 'Don't launch that boat!' cried Romaine. 'There are women and children still aboard.' One of the stokers threatened to strike down the sharp, after which the crewmen swung the boat out and began to lower themselves down to the water. The sharps ran to a lower deck and jumped into the boat as it went by, and the twelve stokers told them to lie down and shut up. The 'sneak boat' was rowed away about half a mile before the crewmen stopped, fearing they would be shot if they were seen. The stokers did not attempt to rescue anyone, and the sharps feared incurring their wrath if they suggested rowing back to pick up swimmers. When daylight came all the lifeboats were picked up except the 'sneak boat', but when the stokers realised they were about to be left behind they rowed towards the *Carpathia* and were finally seen and taken aboard. (It was in this interview the gamblers told of starting a relief fund for the passengers and of attempting to solicit money from Bruce Ismay, so it must be left up to the reader to decide if the story of their relief fund contains any truth.)

Soon after these reports were published, one of the three surviving sharps was found spending his evening in the sitting room of a hotel just off Broadway. The New York underworld was said to be deriving great amusement from the widely varying stories being told about the escape of the *Titanic*'s sharps, so the unnamed gambler (perhaps George Brereton) said he would tell the true story of how he and his confederates escaped with their lives. The gambler's account was greatly abridged by the reporter transcribing it, but it appears to be reliable, with the following possible exception: he said the man they observed being dragged from a lifeboat for the third time went below decks, returned with a revolver and began firing. The gamblers decided they were in a dangerous place, because they could also hear shots coming from another part of the ship.

The sharp's claim to have seen a passenger fire his revolver is completely uncorroborated by other survivors, but the other shots he heard could easily have been those fired by Fifth Officer Harold Lowe. The remainder of the information presented in the interview appears to be an honest account of the gamblers' activities on board the *Titanic*.

On 26 April, a New York correspondent for the *London Daily Chronicle* filed an extraordinary story concerning the gamblers, claiming that, when the *Titanic* sailed from Southampton, notices were already posted in her smoking room warning passengers that professional gamblers were known to be on board. At the time of the collision, Harry Homer, 'Doc' Owen and a third sharp were engaged in a card game. Learning that the ship was doomed, the three men were prevented from entering a lifeboat by the ship's officers, who were allowing only women and children into the boats. Earlier in the voyage the gamblers had paid a certain steward to keep their identity secret, and now they went to him for assistance. In exchange for a roll of banknotes, the steward furnished the three men with women's clothing and hats. Dressed in this garb, the sharps went back on deck and leaped into a lifeboat as it was being lowered. Later, they took off the women's clothes and threw them overboard. Their boat was filled with immigrant women and lacked sufficient men to handle the oars, so the three gamblers assisted in rowing the boat.

A follow-up article concerning the female clothing allegedly worn by the gamblers appeared in the *Western Daily Mercury* on 30 April after *Titanic*'s surviving crewmen arrived back in England:

> One of the crew, who has crossed the Atlantic many times, was openly incredulous regarding the story that some well-known ocean gamblers escaped in women's clothing, which they had bought from stewards, but he admitted that men of that class were on board the *Titanic*, and expressed surprise to find them afterwards on the *Carpathia*.

A couple of days went by with no further word on the gamblers, but early on the morning of 28 April a newspaper reporter encountered 'Doc' Owen in London. Owen was greatly upset about the above report, claiming he had given up the 'steamship graft' forever and that he had not been on board the *Titanic* at all. Owen actually intended to consult his solicitor with a view of bringing a suit against those people who had besmirched his character. (He never did, though.)

At that point the three gamblers dropped out of the limelight in New York City. Charles Romaine and George Brereton probably remained in the city for a while, but Harry Homer left New York and headed west (although it is uncertain if he was really bound for San Antonio, as he wrote to his sister).

Let us leave Harry Homer travelling west for a moment and briefly turn our attention to Denver, Colorado.

During this period Denver was known as the 'Capital of Con' and was ruled by the criminal boss Lou Blonger. For years he had been top man in Denver, paying off the police chief and a vast number of officers so that his confidence games could prosper without interference. His only rule was that his con men must bilk only out-of-town marks and were never to fleece the local people or else public opinion would put their con games out of business. During his peak years, Blonger had 500 con men in his employ, each of whom paid him 50 per cent of their earnings for the privilege of working in the safety of Denver. (This state of affairs undoubtedly had a great deal to do with the fact that Harry Silberberg made a stopover there while on his way to the Pacific coast.)

In 1911 a beautiful woman named Gertrude Patterson was accused of killing her husband in Denver, and a sensational scandal-ridden trial eventually saw her acquitted. It was rumoured at various times that either Emil Strauss of Chicago or *Titanic* passenger Emil Brandeis of Omaha had been infatuated with Mrs Patterson and provided the money that led to her successful legal defence. Strauss and Brandeis had then gone (separately) to Europe and, according to gossip in Chicago, Mrs Patterson had accompanied one or the other of them in their travels. (As it turned out, these rumours were untrue.)

Not long before the *Titanic*'s maiden voyage, Gertrude Patterson reportedly wrote to her parents in Illinois saying she would be returning to the States on board the big White Star liner, but later she sent word that she had changed her mind. After the *Titanic*'s loss, it was widely rumoured that Mrs Patterson really did sail on the ship in company with Emil Strauss, both of them sailing under assumed names. Almost immediately it was said that Patterson and Strauss were still alive in Europe, but then more rumours claimed they had both perished in the disaster. Speculation blew hot and cold as April 1912 drew to a close and May arrived.

Finally, Chicago business partners of Emil Strauss received a letter from him stating that he was still alive in Europe. Since Emil Brandeis was known to have perished on the *Titanic*, the rumours then shifted and claimed it was Brandeis who had been lost with Gertrude Patterson.

In Omaha (the hometown of Emil Brandeis), a man named 'Billy' Nesselhouse received a letter from 'a card player named Martin' who was well known in Omaha. 'Martin' was supposedly a survivor of the *Titanic* disaster, and, although his letter shed no light on Mrs Patterson, it did state that 'Martin' had seen Emil Brandeis in one of *Titanic*'s public rooms shortly before the collision.

It is unknown which of the *Titanic*'s three surviving sharps might have written the letter to 'Billy' Nesselhouse, but on 7 May Harry Homer arrived in Denver and registered at the Brown Palace Hotel. He probably discussed the *Titanic* disaster with a number of people and, in doing so, was made aware of the controversy surrounding the alleged fate of Gertrude Patterson and Emil Brandeis. Homer related what he knew of them from his own first-hand observations:

> I saw Brandeis on the ship when the last boat left the ship's side. I knew him very well and I saw Mrs Patterson several times during her trial. The woman was not on the *Titanic*, or if she was, she did not appear in the first class passenger salon or dining room before the collision or on deck during the excitement which followed.

(Gertrude Patterson was later discovered living incognito in an exclusive Chicago neighbourhood and was never on board the *Titanic*.)

Curiously, after stating what he knew about Emil Brandeis, Harry Homer repeated his story that Henry Harris was playing poker at the time of the collision and was the only one to leave the table to put his wife into a lifeboat. Clearly Harris made a great impression on the sharp, so perhaps Homer was the grifter Harris suspected of cheating in the shipboard poker game.

Homer expressed his intention of remaining in Denver for a few days to look after his investments, and it is here that we temporarily lose track of the three sharps who survived the sinking of the *Titanic*. Even so, there is one additional professional gambler we have not yet discussed, so let us return to Saturday, 20 April 1912. The *Titanic*'s survivors have been in New York City for just thirty-six hours ...

6

JAY YATES

In common with all other American newspapers, the *New York World* was preparing for another day's coverage of the *Titanic* disaster when the day's mail delivery included a certain letter to the editor containing a page torn from a small pocket appointment book that bore a very brief message:

If saved inform my sister Mrs F.J. Adams of Findlay, Ohio. Lost
                                                              — J.H. Rogers

Enclosed with the above note was a short letter:

You will find note that was handed to me as I was leaving the *Titanic*. Am stranger to this man, but think he was a card player. He helped me aboard a lifeboat and I saw him help others. Before we were lowered I saw him jump into the sea. If picked up I did not recognize him on the *Carpathia*. I don't think he was registered on the ship under his own name.

— Survivor

The editor of the *World* discovered that 'J.H. Rogers' was an alias used by Jay Yates, a gambler, confidence man and fugitive from justice, and he took immediate steps to contact Yates's family members in order to inform them of his fate. The *World* had a correspondent in Findlay, Ohio, and this man was instructed to speak with any relatives of Yates that he could find. Apparently, the first person the reporter contacted was Yates's elderly mother, Mrs Mary Yates. When told that her son had perished on the *Titanic*, the poor woman broke down.

'Thank God I know where he is now,' the grief-stricken mother sobbed. 'I have not heard from him for two years. The last news I had from him he was in London. I spent nearly a fortune getting him out of trouble some years ago. Then he was charged with forgery.'

On the afternoon of 21 April, Yates's sister, Mrs Frank J. Adams, granted a brief interview to a local reporter and told him she had not heard from her brother since he dropped her a postcard from New York around 1 February. Mrs Adams was fairly certain Yates was dead, since she had been told that a 'Harry Rogers' was listed among *Titanic*'s second-class passengers and thought this might be her brother (it was not). She also thought it possible that Yates had taken over the booking of a passenger who cancelled his reservation too late for the passenger list to be corrected.

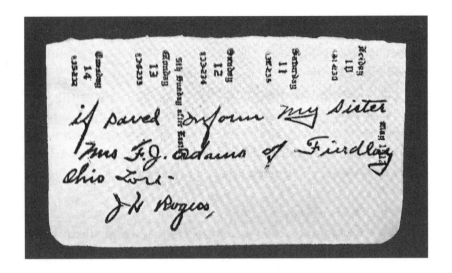

The relatives of Jay Yates hoped to establish beyond all shadow of doubt whether or not he was truly dead. If the death could be proved, Hanna Yates could then begin proceedings to collect upon her husband's life insurance policies.

On 23 April, a reporter showed Mrs Adams a facsimile of the note Yates had written from the *Titanic*. Yates's sister said the note was undoubtedly written in her brother's hand, pointing out the peculiar formation of the letter 'y' in the word 'my' in the note's first line. She said this one characteristic would be enough to convince her that Yates had written the message.

Several Findlay men who knew Yates read the letter that the unnamed survivor had sent to the *New York World* with the note, and they all expressed doubt about the veracity of the story of Yates's death. These men felt the woman's letter was full of inconsistencies – especially the fact that it had been sent anonymously. If the woman had signed the name of a real survivor to her letter the survivor could easily have denied writing it, thus proving the letter to be a fraud, so this awkward possibility was avoided by making the letter anonymous. Another curious point was that the alleged lady survivor believed Yates had been using an alias – something she could not possibly have known had she really been a stranger to him. The fact that she said Yates was also a card player would conveniently have alerted the police, caused them to scrutinise the name 'J.H. Rogers' and connect that alias with Yates. What better way to throw the police off Yates's trail than to let them solve a few minor puzzles as a way of learning the true identity of a man who supposedly died on the *Titanic*?

The members of Yates's family were left in a state of uncertainty. On 27 April a report reached them that, while searching the Atlantic for *Titanic* victims, the cable ship *Mackay-Bennett* had picked up the body of Edward J. Rogers. This was the only name that bore any resemblance to 'J.H. Rogers', but it was not similar enough to permit any kind of certainty in the Yates family, who intended to make enquiries after the morgue ship reached Halifax. If the body proved to be that of Jay Yates, the family planned to have it sent to Findlay for burial. (E.J. Rogers proved to be a member of the *Titanic*'s crew.)

When the first reports of Yates's death were published in Columbus, Ohio, Deputy State Marshal Al Bauer wrote to Inspector W.W. Dickson of the government service in New York asking about the report. On 30 April, Bauer received a reply from Dickson stating very plainly that Yates was not on board the *Titanic* and that 'Doc' Owen was never on the ship either. Dickson was correct about Owen, but he then complicated his report to Marshal Bauer when he said that two other gamblers, 'Old Man' Jordan and 'One-armed' McAuliffe, were on the *Titanic* and that both men were saved.

Since we know 'Old Man' Jordan and Tom McAuliffe were not on board the *Titanic*, these discrepancies introduce an element of doubt regarding the accuracy of Inspector Dickson's pronouncement about Jay Yates. Part of Dickson's report was accurate, part was mistaken and part was of unknown reliability, but Marshal Bauer (who was unaware of that fact) spoke to reporters about the alleged death of Jay Yates. Bauer declared:

> The story is a plain stall, put out by Yates and his associates to throw the government off his trail, but it will fool no one. We have known for some time that Yates was making frequent trips across the Atlantic, operating among the passengers as a gambler, but he would be the last man to be lost. He is utterly heartless and would not hesitate to harm a woman to save his own skin.

Bauer added that a gambler needed protection in order to operate on a ship just as he needed protection to operate in a city. He felt that a White Star Line employee was taking care of the sharp and would slip him a sailor's outfit so that he could take his place in one of the *Titanic's* lifeboats.

And so, with this final published report, the name 'Jay Yates' briefly dropped from the newspaper headlines. It can be assumed that the Yates family hoped Marshal Bauer was correct about Yates being alive in New York, but the uncertainty and mental strain on the family members, especially Yates's mother, must have been great.

Public interest in the *Titanic* disaster quietened down, and the general public forgot all about Jay Yates. But on 13 June 1912, Findlay, Ohio's *Hancock Courier* published an article claiming that Yates (alias 'Albert Berger') and a fellow con artist named James Burkert had just been captured in Baltimore. According to one newspaper report:

> At Baltimore Berger or Yates secured $100 in cash from the clerk of the Hotel Rennert by means of a bogus money order, and $40 and a traveling bag valued at $20 from C.J. Dunn, on a similar bogus order. Burkert, his pal, got $100 from W.H.J. Culp, a clerk in a Baltimore jewelry store.

Postal inspector Major S. Thornton arrested Albert Berger and James Burkert on 9 June 1912, but both men refused to make a statement. Former inspector Frank Oldfield identified Berger as Yates and, in his daily report to the US Secret Service, operative Charles Wright wrote:

> Berger is supposed to be J.T. Yates, who is wanted all over the country, California and other Western states for passing forged money orders ... If this man Berger is J.T. Yates, there is about 27 indictments against him at Columbus, Ohio.

Albert Berger and James Burkert were scheduled to be arraigned on 17 June 1912, and their photographs and Bertillon measurements were taken and sent all over the country for further identification. One newspaper wrote, 'It is believed that the men are wanted also in Cincinnati, Chicago, Indianapolis, St. Louis, Los Angeles, San Francisco and Boston as well as Columbus.'

According to researcher Patrick Fitch:

> On June 21, 1912, acting on the advice of his attorney, Berger pleaded guilty to the charges against him and was sentenced to five years' imprisonment at the Atlanta Georgia Federal Penitentiary. After serving three years of his sentence, Berger died of heart failure on the prison's recreation grounds at 2.45 p.m. on October 23, 1915.

Unfortunately, the notion that Albert Berger was actually Jay Yates turned out to be a case of mistaken identity, because on 12 July 1912, Ralph Miller, secretary to Findlay's Mayor E.L. Groves, wrote to Baltimore's chief of police on behalf of Yates's mother asking if Berger was indeed him. On 15 July 1912, the United States Marshal Service wrote the following reply:

I am in receipt of your letter of 12th instant respecting Jay Yates, and to say in reply thereto that the two men arrested in Baltimore gave their names as Albert Berger and James Burkert. It was at first thought that Berger was in reality Yates, but subsequent developments proved to the contrary. Both men have been sentenced and are now confined in the Federal Prison at Atlanta, Georgia.

After June 1912 the name 'Jay Yates' disappeared from the daily newspapers, and the months gradually turned into years. The Great Depression arrived and dragged on. It was 1932.

Wallace B. Yates was living in Findlay, Ohio, at that time, he being a descendant of Jasper N. Yates, one of Jay's half-brothers. Wallace succeeded in gaining employment at Findlay Hospital where, coincidentally, Hanna Yates (Yates's wife) also worked. One day they were talking together when the subject of Hanna's husband came up, and Hanna told Wallace that six or eight months had gone by after the *Titanic* disaster when, one night around midnight, a man came up to the door of her home on West Pearl Street. It was Jay Yates.

Sometime after the disaster, Yates had sent word to Hanna that he had been rescued and was safe, but this was the first time she had seen him in person since the sinking of the *Titanic*. Hanna seemed to think he was in some kind of trouble, because he only stayed with her for a few hours before leaving again early the next morning. Hanna never saw Yates again.

The last time Wallace Yates spoke with Hanna was in 1936 and, after that, we do not know what happened to her. She must have been getting on in years, but her future activities, like those of her husband, remain unknown.

On 25 January 1913 (shortly after her husband's nocturnal visit to her home), Hanna Yates filed a petition for divorce against Jay Yates in the Court of Common Pleas, Hancock County, Ohio. The petition was granted on 20 March 1913, and Hanna was restored to her maiden name of Williams. She also received the property on Lima Avenue that she and Yates had called their residence, and she then sold that property for $2,350.

During the First World War, two men from Carbon, Indiana, returned to Findlay and told members of the Yates family that they had recently seen and spoken with Yates in London. Nothing seems to have been heard from him when his mother passed away on 3 August 1919, but when his sister, Mrs Frank Adams, passed away in 1923 the family was led to believe by a relative that a mysterious phone call received at that time was from Yates.

In 2016, newspaperman Senan Molony wrote an article disparaging author Walter Lord's 1955 belief that Yates was a genuine *Titanic* passenger. He went on to report that Yates was not on board the *Titanic* and that in 1915 Yates died in prison under the alias 'A.P. Berger'. However, the present author published a 1982 *Commutator* article proving that Yates was never on the *Titanic*, while Patrick Fitch proved conclusively, in the January 2000 edition of the same magazine, that the man who died in prison in 1915 was not him.

The present writer made an enquiry to the US Postal Inspector asking if Yates was ever captured for his theft of the postal money orders, but no response was ever received. And so, for the time being, the facts in the story of Yates have trickled to a stop.

Before we conclude our discussion of Jay Yates, let us look briefly at a couple of puzzling references that (on the surface) might suggest that Yates was a real *Titanic* passenger who secretly survived the disaster.

On 3 May 1912, one of the *Titanic*'s three surviving gamblers (probably George Brereton) was still in New York City when he spoke with Tom Costello of Cincinnati about his experiences during the sinking. 'Sunday night we were in the card room playing cards with a passenger whose name I do not know,' the sharp explained to

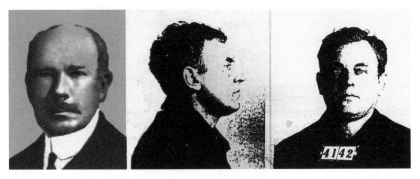

Jay Yates (left) and Albert Berger (right).

Costello. 'Besides myself there was a gambler who hails from Ohio, and another from Indianapolis.'

The unnamed gambler from Indianapolis was clearly Harry Homer, who used his sister's Indianapolis home as his base of operations, but the identity of the other gambler is more puzzling as neither George Brereton nor Charles Romaine was from Ohio. (In 1880 Romaine worked as a farm labourer in Ohio, but in 1892 he moved to Indiana.) However, Jay Yates was from Findlay, Ohio, a fact that coincides with the *Titanic* sharp's description of one of his unnamed gambling partners. Might this mean that Yates was truly on board the *Titanic*?

An interesting story that might pertain to this topic was told by Alice Silvey, a *Titanic* survivor who lost her husband in the sinking. As she was entering her lifeboat Mrs Silvey injured her ankle by stepping on a man who was hiding under a seat; in her first interview she merely called the man a stowaway, but in a later interview she said the following:

When getting into the lifeboat I stepped on a man who was lying underneath the seats. After we were aboard the *Carpathia* I met him face to face. He was a gambler, I think, and sneaked away from me as if he were ashamed of the fact that he was among the living.

Alice Silvey.

Whether or not Alice Silvey was correct in calling this unknown man a gambler will never be known, but might he have been Yates? The argument that disproves this intriguing suggestion is the simple fact that we know the true name and background of every male passenger who travelled in first class on board the *Titanic*. Jay Yates was not one of them.

We have already mentioned a reference to a professional gambler seen by second-class survivor Madeleine Mellinger, who wrote to Walter Lord describing the way she and her mother reached the boat deck:

We were on E deck. The one reason to mention the fact that the elevator was not running but I remember for we had to walk up all those stairs. On the way up we met a beautiful man who had made friends with me. He was a professional gambler. He told mother he had had a big night (?) and I wondered what he [meant] until she told me what he was. I thought he was grand (me 13 years old).

138

Madeleine Mellinger.

Professional gamblers usually booked as first-class passengers on ocean liners for the simple reason that wealthy passengers were more lucrative targets than were average citizens. However, Madeleine Mellinger and her mother were both second-class passengers on the *Titanic*, which meant it was unlikely that a gambler travelling in first class would have had any opportunity to befriend young Miss Mellinger in second class. Does this mean an unknown gambler might have been travelling in second class on the *Titanic*, and might this gambler have been Yates? The name of the supposed gambler in second class may never be known, but – once again – we know the true name and background of every male passenger who travelled in second class on the *Titanic*. Jay Yates was not one of them.

7

THE THREE SURVIVING GAMBLERS

The time has come for us to briefly summarise what little is known of the subsequent lives of the three professional gamblers who were on board the *Titanic* during her maiden voyage and survived the sinking.

HARRY HOMER

Harry Homer had no intention of walking away from the *Titanic* disaster with nothing to show for it except the shirt on his back, and, using his alias of 'H. Haven', he filed a $2,500 claim with the White Star Line for his lost baggage. Later in 1912, 'H.H. Homer' made an Atlantic crossing on board the White Star liner *Olympic* and also booked under that name for another *Olympic* voyage in 1913. During that same year, a Harry Homer from Indianapolis boarded the liner *France* and arrived in New York on 26 September, and in 1914 a man of the same name boarded the *Mauretania* in Liverpool and arrived in New York on 13 March.

On 14 April 1914, Homer arrived in New York on the *Rotterdam*, and in Manhattan on 17 April he married again, this time to Marie Maud Hanscom (born 28 June 1883), a divorcee from Akron, Ohio, who embraced his illegal lifestyle. (Although there is evidence the couple may have lived in Cincinnati and Los Angeles during the

Harry Homer.

1920s and 1930s, other indications suggest that Marie may have died as early as 1920.) A few days later, 'Henry Homer' boarded the *Olympic* in New York and arrived in Southampton on 25 April.

In August 1914, the outbreak of the First World War caused Homer to begin a six-year hiatus in his overseas travels, but during that same month 'Harry Baldwin' (Harry Homer), 'George A. Banning' (George Brereton) and three confederates ran a wanted advert in the *Detroit News-Tribune* advertising that they wanted to invest in Michigan farmland. Oakland County's Wilbur Rundle had 200 acres he wanted to sell and was one of two farmers who responded to the advert. One thing led to another, and eventually, in Toledo, Ohio, Rundle was fleeced for $3,000 in a horse-racing wire-tap scheme. Rundle went to the authorities and, in January 1915, Brereton and Homer were fined $2,000 each for using the mails in connection with a confidence game and were sentenced to serve two years in the Moundsville, West Virginia Penitentiary (one report says the federal penitentiary in Atlanta, Georgia). Harry made the appeal bond of $5,000 but then skipped town.

To the San Francisco Police Department, Harry Homer had the reputation of being a 'swell mobsman', a thief who operated only in society and high-class circles, and in 1915 a San Francisco fruit dealer named Peter Mokovihs was drawn into Homer's clutches when he met a beautiful blonde who pretended to be infatuated with him. The woman lured Mokovihs first to Los Angeles and then to San Diego, where she introduced him to Homer and several of his confederates. Homer told Mokovihs about a wiretapping scheme that would enable him to make a fortune, and the fruit dealer was subsequently permitted to win $20,000 before the beautiful blonde convinced him to return to San Francisco to get $8,000 of his own money. Mokovihs did so but, at that point, his 'luck' took a turn for the worse when Homer lowered the boom by winning back the $20,000 plus the fruit dealer's own $8,000.

On 30 September 1915, Homer was arrested in San Francisco for perpetrating the wiretap scheme on Peter Mokovihs. Interestingly, Homer's wife, a beautiful blonde reputed to be the daughter of a wealthy Toledo banker, was also arrested in the belief she was the decoy who lured Mokovihs into Homer's clutches.

In November 1915, Homer was arrested in Chicago, where the city's newspapers duly recorded the event:

> Harry Homer, said by the police to have a long criminal record, was taken into custody yesterday by detectives who told him he was suspected of planning to work a wiretapping game on Maj. B. Shaw Wood of the British army, who is at the Congress hotel seeking supplies in Chicago for his government. Homer was told that two other men – known as 'English Jim' and Rothbart – were in the conspiracy with him. He denied knowing these men. He said he had bought a ticket for Cleveland when he read of the plot with which he was credited. The police are thinking of something to charge him with.

Homer eventually became the 'big loop' in a gang of seven con men that operated in Oklahoma, Texas, Arkansas, Kansas and Missouri. His team of grifters concentrated on mulcting victims in the smaller towns of Oklahoma and Texas, but they also welcomed occasional opportunities to relieve rich Tulsa and Oklahoma City citizens of their superfluous wealth.

It was probably late in 1918 that the team of grifters was operating in Wichita, Kansas, and successfully swindled two farmers out of the $35,000 they put up for the purchase of copper stocks. Using the alias 'C.H. Brewster', Homer also ran up debts of several thousand dollars in Oklahoma City before absconding and leaving those debts unpaid, which caused the local authorities to begin a search for the fleeing grifter.

Harry Homer in 1919.

Early in 1919, Harry Homer (using the name 'J.H. Logsdon', his sister's married name) was in Mineral Wells, Texas, where he made the acquaintance of Joseph Williams, a past sheriff of Francois County and owner of a very fine farm. 'Logsdon' told Williams he was the son of a rich Tulsa oil producer and his parents wanted to buy a good farm and retire from the oil game to live the quiet life. Williams offered to sell his farm to them for $52,000, and 'Logsdon' suggested that they travel to Tulsa the following week to talk with his family about the proposed purchase. At that time, Logsdon's rich 'father' was supposed to turn the earnest money for the farm over to Williams.

On 17 March, the day Williams was supposed to meet with 'Logsdon', a woman called at his hotel while he was out but left the hotel without leaving a message or returning. Later that day, the entire deal was interrupted when 'Logsdon' was arrested in Mineral Springs, Texas, based on information provided by the authorities in Oklahoma City. Deputy US Marshal John Alerman and Fort Worth, Texas's assistant chief of police, C.H. Young, escorted Homer to

Toledo, Ohio, and the custody of the city's federal court, and he was then placed in the Lucas County jail.

On 28 March, when asked by the police where the rest of his seven-member gang was hiding, Homer spoke about a supposed gambling house located on East Tenth Street in Tulsa. He then boasted that if he had been permitted to continue his con game, he would have mulcted Joseph Williams out of $50,000. The talkative con man said he had arranged to meet Williams in Mineral Wells, Texas, and take him to a Tulsa gambling house, where a wiretap game would convince Williams to accept an 'oil lease' in exchange for his Missouri farm. (Homer was said to have blushed when he made this admission to his captors, because he was embarrassed about working a con game as old and well known as this one.) Homer did not seem worried about his present capture, though, and he jocularly greeted various Toledo police officers and called them by their first names. A local reporter noted:

> Pikers were barred [from his con games], Homer told the officers, and there were no rules or limits to the games. It was a gentleman's game, and now that he has lost, Homer smokes his cigar in the Lucas County jail in reflective silence. He will talk about his exploits but will not give his pals away. Asked for the address of the Tenth street gambling house in Tulsa he only smiled and said, 'I can't remember'.

When he was pressed to reveal the Tulsa gambling house's specific address, Homer finally claimed it was located at 710 East Tenth Street. Upon being asked if any gang members were still in Tulsa, he replied, 'There were two there a week ago. I don't know where they are now. They are clever boys and the officers will be lucky to get them.'

Unsurprisingly, it turned out that the address he provided was a false one, and Deputy Marshal John Moran told reporters it was unlikely Homer would ever give any information that might lead to the capture of his confederates. It was stated that Homer would be taken to the prison in Atlanta to serve his two-year term plus any extra time that Federal Judge Killoth decided to tack onto his sentence because of the bond-jumping charge.

In June 1920, Homer recommenced his ocean travels when he booked passage under his own name on the *Minnedosa* and, during the next two years, additional voyages were to take place on the *Nieuw Amsterdam*, *Berengeria*, *Aquitania*, *Olympic*, *Mauretania* and *Homeric*. In 1921 Harry applied for an American passport, and in 1923 he applied for another passport for the stated purpose of travelling to France, Belgium and England for business and pleasure. His paperwork described him as being 5ft 9in tall with brown hair, blue eyes and a fair complexion.

In June 1923, Homer left Cherbourg on the *Majestic*, arriving in New York on the 19th, but that arrival seems to have initiated another of his lengthy hiatuses from ocean voyaging.

In May 1926, a San Francisco newspaper described Homer's latest brush with the law:

Two men arrested in the same downtown hotel yesterday are held by the police on suspicion that they are wanted in other cities as confidence men.

A middle-aged prosperous looking man who was known at the hotel as Charles W. Baker, an Australian, is believed by detectives to be J.B. Kinsman, wanted in Denver and Okmulgee, Okla. as a 'high class bunk man' and for whom a $1000 reward.

Later detectives Frank McConnell and Charles Gallivan also arrested Harry H. Homer, who claimed to be an Indiana farmer, but who police say is wanted in Los Angeles and New York. He admitted having been arrested during the exposition in 1915 on a vagrancy charge and said he had once been a bookmaker but now devoted all his time to farming.

Each of the men had about $300 when arrested and both were unusually well dressed.

On 26 July 1930, 'Henry H. Homer' of Knightstown, Indiana, boarded the liner *Empress of France* at Cherbourg and made the crossing to New York. Homer gave his current city of residence as Sharonville, Ohio, and travelling with him on the *Empress* was his old partner in crime, George A. Brereton.

On 14 February 1931, Homer arrived in New York from Cherbourg on the *Europa* and, during the next four years, he made additional voyages on the *President Garfield*, *President McKinley*, *Leviathan*, *Yasukuni Maru*, *Europa*, *Bremen* and several other vessels.

In July 1935, Homer boarded the White Star liner MV *Britannic* at Le Havre, France, and arrived in New York on 21 July, his home address being listed as 270 West End Avenue, New York City.

Harry Homer during his senior years.

At this point, the public trail left by 64-year-old Harry Haven Homer begins to fade away, but researcher Philip Gowan once corresponded with members of the present-day Homer family and learned some interesting things about Harry's ice-cold heart and uncaring nature. Gowan writes:

> When Homer's wife died, he had her cremated and mailed the ashes to his brother who lived on a farm near Cincinnati. There was a note attached from him that didn't tell his brother what was in the package but just asked him to keep the package until he came for his next visit. He didn't show up in Cincinnati again for another two years and when he did, he didn't even bother to ask what happened to the package he had sent. Fortunately, his brother had figured it out and had buried Mrs Homer on the family plot.

One additional lead about Homer's later life comes in the form of an obituary of Mrs Louise LeGassick that was published in the *Los Angeles Times* on 21 September 1936. Mrs LeGassick was the former Louise Logsdon of Indianapolis, and her obituary describes her as being the 'sister of Harry Homer of New York and Ed Homer of Los Angeles; also survived by one sister in the East'. We therefore know that Harry Homer and his brother Ed were both still alive in 1936 and that Harry was still based in New York at that time.

During his twilight years, Harry Homer resided for a time in Hamilton, Ohio, but on 10 February 1939 he passed away in Manhattan, New York. His estate was left to his brother Morris and the latter's wife Emma, who lived in Butler, Ohio.

One last puzzle connected with Harry Homer dates from 29 September 1939 (seven months after his death), at which time the *Knightstown Banner* published an article stating that William Homer (one of Harry's elder brothers) had come to town to visit his old friends. The intriguing thing about this report is that historian Don

Lynch has seen evidence suggesting that William Homer had passed away six years previously in 1933. Before Harry Homer's death date was determined with certainty, Lynch initially believed that Harry might have been travelling under his brother's name in 1939. However, if Harry was dead by September 1939 – and if his brother William died in 1933 – who was the 'William Homer' who came to town to visit his old friends? (Based on Harry's elusive nature throughout his lifetime, we are tempted to wonder if he might somehow have given the Grim Reaper the slip and was still travelling the country using an easily remembered alias.)

CHARLES ROMAINE

Charles Romaine's life continued in its usual way after he survived the *Titanic* disaster and, just like Harry Homer, he filed a $2,500 baggage claim against the White Star Line (and for good measure tacked on a $5,000 claim for personal injuries). On 2 February 1913, Romaine (travelling under his own name) arrived in New York from Southampton on board the liner *Amerika*.

At some point (one report says 1915), Romaine reportedly moved to London and spent several years there as the managing director of the Throg-Morton Trust Company. (Contradictory reports vary as to whether this move to London took place in the 1890s or if it happened after the *Titanic* disaster, since it is sometimes claimed that Romaine lived in London for thirteen years.) In any case, in 1916 he is said to have returned to New York and engaged in a banking (some say brokerage) business there. He was reputed to be popular among his many friends in New York City, and his passport from the year before describes him as being 5ft 11in tall with grey hair, brown eyes and a dark complexion.

Charles Romaine.

In corresponding with members of the present-day Romaine family, researcher Philip Gowan learned things that gave him a fair idea of the type of man Romaine really was. Gowan agrees that Harry Homer and George Brereton both had 'souls of ice', but in regard to Charles Romaine he writes:

Romaine is a different story. True, he traveled the seas to swindle the rich people, but he was a friendly, gregarious man and beloved by all that knew him in his everyday life back in the United States. He was kind to his wife and relatives and those that knew him well only had good things to say about him. As late as a couple of years ago [2005] he still had a niece alive in her late 90s and she had wonderful stories to tell about her uncle 'Hallace.' While Brereton and Homer didn't seem bothered at all by their *Titanic* experience, Romaine only traveled a very few times afterwards and for the most part stopped his gambling. So I think in him you would have found a lot more soul and some decency.

In 2002, 90-year-old Ann Harris (Romaine's only living relative who remembered him) recalled:

> I was about 5 years [old] when I last saw him. I remember him clearly, because he was something else. He was quite handsome. He had beautiful white hair. When he came to visit, my mother and grandmother made a fuss for days preparing for his arrival. I adored him. He was supposed to be a stock broker; that was what I was told.

In 1920 Romaine and his wife Doll appeared on the census as residing at 315 West 98th Street in Manhattan, and he was described as being a promoter of oil stocks.

On 21 May 1921, Charles H. Romaine filed a bankruptcy petition in New York City, with no assets and liabilities of $6,205. At that time, he was described as being a former banker who 'had been out of active business for several years' even though he was only 54 years of age.

Just eight months later, the name of Charles H. Romaine again appeared in print. On the evening of 18 January 1922, Romaine started out for a walk through the city, but as he stepped into the street a taxi came speeding around the corner and struck him down. He was rushed to a hospital but was pronounced dead of a compound skull fracture. His wife was away from their apartment at the time and did not learn of his death until later. William Reilly, the taxi driver, was arrested on a homicide charge because he was speeding at the time of the accident.

Charles Romaine was survived by three brothers, R.A. Romine; Frank Romine, of Anderson; Henry Romine, of Cincinnati; two sisters, Mrs John Fynney and Mrs O.L. Pierce. (The spelling of the Romaine name varied in the family.) His widow Doll never remarried and later settled in Englewood, New Jersey. She died in January 1970 at the age of 95 and was buried next to her husband.

GEORGE BRERETON

After the *Titanic* disaster, George Brereton (using his alias 'George Brayton') filed the following claim for losses against the Oceanic Steam Navigation Company:

$22.00	1 solid gold chain
$3.50	1 golf cap
$24.00	1/2 doz. dress shirts
$36.00	flannel shirts
$18.00	negligee
$40.00	4 pr. silk pajamas
$60.00	1/2 doz. suits silk and wool Uwear
$48.00	2 doz. silk hose
$27.00	3 doz, Hdcf
$6.00	2 doz. collars
$48.00	2 doz. cravats
$18.00	Golf bag and sticks
$60.00	Gold knife and pencil
$85.00	1 Hartman Wardrobe Trunk
$25.00	1 hat box
$125.00	1 bag with silver fittings
$35.00	1 leather hand bag
$60.00	1 Eastman camera with Goertz Lens
$400.00	1 case scarf pins
$65.00	1 solid gold watch
$60.00	1 pair gold cuff buttons diamond set
$55.00	1 set binoculars
$60.00	1 set full dress studs pearls
$95.00	1 fob chain (small diamonds)
$125.00	1 gold ring (5 small diamonds)
$16.00	1 silk umbrella – silver handle

$54.00	3 walking sticks
$400.00	1 mink lined overcoat
$80.00	1 light top coat
$125.00	1 full dress suit
$90.00	1 tuxedo suit
$360.00	6 lounge suits
$65.00	1 Norfolk suit
$65.00	1 riding suit
$55.00	1 white flannel suit
$80.00	1 walking suit
$25.00	1 pair riding boots
$12.00	1 dress shoes
$42.00	6 pair shoes
$5.00	1 silk opera hat
$6.00	1 silk hat
$5.00	1 black derby
1 leather wallet with U.S. and English currency	
$1,100.00	U.S. currency
£20	English Bank Notes (U.S. $98.00)

$4,283.50 TOTAL

On 10 May 1912, Nelson White (a relative of *Titanic* victims Percival White and his son Richard) wrote a letter to survivor 'George Brayton' asking if the latter had any contact with his late relatives during the maiden voyage. On 12 May, 'Brayton' wrote a surprisingly courteous reply to Mr White (possibly with the intent of cultivating him and setting him up for a later con job):

Yours of the 10th inst. to hand and in reply will say that the inquiry of any news of Percival W. White and Richard F. White I am only glad to give. I remember them both very well as they dined at an adjoining table to me so I not only saw them on deck but also at mealtime. I saw them both after the Titanic struck and they were both fully dressed and had life belts on. The elder Mr White was doing all that could be done to help the women and children into the lifeboats and seemed very cool. I was put on one of the last boats to leave and that was the last I saw of them, but on board of the Carpathia I saw several that had to jump in the water and I saw a man that told me he saw them in the water and that he saw the elder Mr White go down. That was the last I heard of them. I am not positive but I think the one that last saw them, that is in the water, was Mr A.H. Barkworth-Hessle, East Yorkshire, Great Britain. That is all the information that I can give you and I certainly hope this will help you to get in touch with the one that saw them in the water. I want to express my sincerest sympathy for your terrible loss and hope that you will call on me if I can be of any further assistance.

Respectfully,
Geo. A. Brayton

George Brereton.

The *Titanic* disaster did not cause George Brereton to miss a beat in conducting his usual confidence games on shore, and by June 1912 he and his confederates had already swindled W.J. Mason, of Norfolk, Virginia, out of $20,000 in New York by using the 'wiretapping' game. Brereton then turned his attention back to *Titanic* survivor Charles Stengel and began making plans to use the same con on him as well.

On 3 June 1912, 'George Brayton' phoned Charles Stengel to renew their acquaintance and said that his brother-in-law, Mr MacDonald, had just returned from Mexico and was now in a position to make some money. Brereton and Stengel met by appointment and went to the local Western Union office where the brother-in-law supposedly had his office. Upon their reaching the fourth floor, a man wearing a green visor hurried past them and Brereton called out 'Hello, Mac!' MacDonald was supposedly too busy to talk with Stengel and Brereton but agreed to meet them at the Hotel Saville for lunch. Stengel then accompanied Brereton to a fourth-floor hotel room where the gambler said he had been staying for the past week, despite the fact that no luggage was visible in the room.

While they waited there for MacDonald to arrive, Brereton told Charles Stengel about a scheme his brother-in-law had devised that was expected to bring in $100,000. When MacDonald came in, he explained that he was in charge of Western Union's 'R.D.' department, which handled horse-racing results from across the country. He then revealed that he could withhold the results of races for at least eight minutes, which would give Brereton and Stengel time to bet on horses that had already won their races. MacDonald even had a racing chart with him and pointed out the horses that were expected to win certain races, and he vowed to donate $1,000 to the pool and wanted Brereton and Stengel to both chip in as well.

Charles Stengel was not a complete babe-in-the-woods and knew all about how this venerable horse-racing con game was operated, and he immediately began to punch MacDonald without mercy. When Brereton begged Stengel not to 'squeal' on them, Stengel began to punch him too. He then went outside and waited for the two gamblers to appear on the street but, when they failed to do so, Stengel contacted the police about the attempted sting and the newspapers found out about it soon afterwards.

On 13 August 1912, George A. Brereton married Zurah A. ('Grace') Heron in Manhattan, New York. Researcher Mike Herbold has determined that Brereton listed his occupation as 'broker' on the marriage certificate and that his brother William served as witness to the ceremony.

As was mentioned earlier, in August 1914, 'George A. Banning' (George Brereton), 'Harry Baldwin' (Harry Homer) and three confederates ran a wanted advert in the *Detroit News-Tribune* advertising that they wanted to invest in Michigan farmland. Oakland County's Wilbur Rundle had 200 acres he wanted to sell and was one of two farmers who responded to the advert. One thing led to another and, eventually, Rundle was fleeced in Toledo for $3,000 in a horse-racing wiretap scheme. Rundle went to the authorities and, on 29 January 1915, Brereton (using the alias 'George Banning') was arrested in Toledo, Ohio, and sentenced to pay a $2,000 fine and serve two years in prison at the Moundsville, West Virginia Penitentiary. Brereton's friend Harry Homer (who used the pseudonyms 'Bolder' and 'Baldwin') received the same fine and sentence, while their three co-conspirators received lesser sentences.

The 1915 census shows George and Grace Brereton to be living in New York, and researcher Mike Herbold has discovered that on 1 December 1917, George Brereton registered for the First World War draft using the alias 'George Arthur Bell'. His wife's name was listed as 'Grace Bell', and their residence was listed as 6508 Ellis Avenue in Chicago.

In Illinois on 10 July 1918, George and Grace Brereton had a son who they named George Daniel Brereton, but on 2 March 1921 the young boy passed away during a tonsillectomy operation.

During one of his many ocean voyages, Brereton met a woman named Hazel Rell (born 16 October 1895), whose parents in Wisconsin were sending her and her sisters to England in hopes that she would find a 'royal' to marry following the collapse of her first marriage. Instead of finding a royal, Hazel Rell found George Brereton. The gambler's duplicitous nature made it impossible for him to be honest with Rell's parents, because, as far as they knew, Brereton (who always spoke with a British accent while in their presence) was 'Sir George Brereton'. (Sadly, that same alias appeared on the death certificate of Brereton's young son.)

On 23 February 1922, Grace Brereton died at the age of 34, but there may have been far more to her death than first meets the eye. Two days after Grace's death, it was reported in the newspapers that Hazel Rell had been sitting with Grace in a home at 7217 Walnut Drive that belonged to Brereton's sister Emily. According to Rell,

Hazel Brereton.

Grace was suddenly overcome with grief over the death of her son, rushed into her bedroom, locked the door and shot herself in the heart with a revolver. Rell later said she heard the shot and ran screaming to a neighbour's home, and the police were called. Grace Brereton's body was found on her bed with the revolver at her side.

In light of what was to happen just a few weeks later, researchers Phil Gowan and Mike Herbold speculate that Grace Brereton might possibly have been a victim of foul play at the hands of Hazel Rell. On the other hand, the present writer wonders if Rell might possibly have made a devastating revelation to Grace about her husband's love life that caused Grace's already fragile mind to despair and seek immediate escape from its pain. At any rate, within just a few weeks of Grace Brereton's death, George Brereton and Hazel Rell were married and moved to 219 E. Olive Street in Huntington Park, California.

In 1923 and 1925, George Brereton made passport applications to the government, his occupation being listed as 'secretary' and his height being 5ft 9in, brown hair, grey eyes, a fresh complexion, 'heavy' chin, and a regular forehead and mouth topped with a moustache. Researcher Mike Herbold has determined that Brereton (and often his wife Hazel) spent a great deal of time at sea — at least thirty different voyages; the gambler took trips from the East Coast through Panama to California; he took cruises back and forth from California to Hawaii; and he took one long trip from the Philippines to British Columbia.

Hazel and George Brereton were destined to have a stormy marital relationship and, since Hazel could not have children of her own, they adopted a son (said to be the out-of-wedlock child of a well-known movie star) and named him Daniel Rell Brereton (born in Los Angeles on 20 July 1927). Eventually, Hazel and George Brereton were divorced.

George Brereton.

On 26 July 1930, Brereton boarded the *Empress of France* at Cherbourg and made the crossing to New York in the company of his old friend and fellow gambler Harry Homer. Brereton listed his home address as 6648 Ellis Avenue in Chicago, and the census listed him as being president of a finance company.

In 1932 George Brereton was 58 years old, but his skill as a bunco artist was still well honed from a lifetime of practice. In that year, a retired New Yorker named J.T. Taylor made the acquaintance of Brereton and a confederate named C.W. Coleman in Yosemite National Park, and eventually the two grifters relieved Taylor of $27,000 using the old racehorse wiretap scheme. Taylor searched for the two bunco men for the next year and, in July 1933, a friend tipped him off that he had spotted the two grifters in Yosemite again. Both con men were members of the Maybury Gang (which had existed since before 1909), so Sheriff William Emig and a group of park rangers obtained the necessary warrants and moved in on their quarry. George Brereton and his partner in crime were arrested in Yosemite at dawn on 4 July 1933, and both men were placed in the

George Brereton.

San Jose County Jail in lieu of $30,000 bail each. Newspapers noted that one of the two expensive automobiles being used by the grifters bore licence plates that had been issued to 'Mrs. H.R. Brerton' (George's wife, Hazel Rell Brereton), and both con men admitted to having used dozens of aliases all over the country.

In 1937 Edward Bacon, the head of a San Francisco machinery firm, was on a round-the-world tour and, while on an Australian golf course, he struck up a friendly acquaintance with a man named Vincent Kenny. Upon boarding the liner *Lurline* to return to the United States, Bacon was surprised to discover that his new friend was also on board, and Kenny immediately introduced Bacon to his friends John Lane and George Brereton. On that first night at sea, the four men began playing a friendly game of 'top-off' to pass the time, and, although Bacon won $38 at the card table that first night, he lost heavily for the rest of the voyage and was in debt to the gamblers to the tune of $9,200 by the time the *Lurline* docked in San Francisco. Bacon did not have that much money with him, so he told Brereton and his two confederates that he would get the money from his bank and would bring it back to the ship. Instead of going to the bank, however, Bacon repaired to the San Francisco Police Department and talked things over with the bunco squad. When Bacon returned to the *Lurline* he pointed out Brereton and his confederates to police officers, and the three grifters were arrested on Christmas Eve and held on $1,000 bail.

On the morning of 11 April 1939, George Brereton and Vincent (Lord) Kelly were once again arrested by the San Francisco Police on suspicion that they had designs on visitors at the San Francisco World's Fair on Treasure Island. The two grifters were subjected to a line-up for the benefit of Exposition police to enable them to be easily recognised if they should show their faces at the fair.

The 1940 census shows George Brereton living in an apartment on Wilshire Boulevard in Los Angeles, with his profession listed as being in the mining sector. George and his sister, Emily Lathrop, were always close to each other, and in 1942 and in later years the 67-year-old grifter was living at Emily's home at 7021 Miramonte Boulevard in Los Angeles, his occupation now being listed as 'car salesman'.

At 7.40 a.m. on 16 July 1942, 'retired real estate broker' George A. Brereton took his own life by putting a 12-gauge shotgun to his head and pulling the trigger. It was his sister Emily who found his body, which was buried in Valhalla Memorial Park in Los Angeles.

After her divorce from George Brereton, Hazel Rell Brereton married a Maytag heir and lived to be a very old woman, dying in California on 18 December 1983. Researcher Phil Gowan writes that George and Hazel's adopted son, Danny, turned out to be 'a very unsavory character. He died a year before his mother, and those responsible for the estate were reluctant to even enter his house, afraid of what they might find.'

8

GAMBLER LEGENDS

Several legends exist concerning confidence men who claimed to have been on the *Titanic*. One of these is mentioned in a book by Jay Nash, titled *Hustlers and Con Men*, and is represented as being factual regarding its *Titanic* connection, even though it is not. Briefly stated, Alvin Clarence Thomas was a notorious con man in the early decades of the twentieth century who was better known by his professional nickname, 'Titanic Thompson'. According to Nash's story, Thompson was one of a group of sharps who boarded the *Titanic* and began fleecing passengers during the crossing.

'Titanic Thompson'.

After the collision occurred, Thompson and three of his colleagues managed to slip into the lifeboats and were rescued, the other three surviving gamblers being the 'Hashhouse Kid', 'Indiana Harry' and 'Hoosier Harry'. After reaching New York, the four sharps supposedly filed maximum property loss claims against the White Star Line to cover their lost personal effects, and they also provided the names of *Titanic* victims to fellow con men to enable them to get a piece of the action as well.

Jay Nash is the only person to claim that 'Titanic Thompson' was on board the *Titanic*, because all other sources contradict that legend. In truth, Thompson acquired his odd nickname in a pool hall right after the loss of the great liner when friends said his pool opponents 'went down like the *Titanic*'. The nickname stuck.

It almost seems that 'Titanic Thompson's' fictional presence on the *Titanic* was tacked onto a garbled version of the story of the three surviving gamblers, since it is a curious coincidence that Nash's story has three other gamblers being saved, two of them being nicknamed 'Harry'. The nicknames 'Indiana Harry' and 'Hoosier

Harry' might refer to either Charles 'Harry' Romaine (Anderson, Indiana) or Harry Homer (Indianapolis, Indiana). As for the claim that the *Titanic*'s gamblers attempted to mulct the White Star Line for maximum damages, readers can look back at George Brereton's claimed property losses and judge the value of his lost belongings for themselves.

Our second gambler legend was apparently known for years among professional card men and was finally put down on paper in 1939 by Michael MacDougall in his book *Gamblers Don't Gamble*. The little melodrama might have made an interesting short story in a book of fiction, because it is certainly an imaginary account.

Briefly, a famous card mechanic named 'Baldy' Johnson was said to have sailed on the *Titanic* with two colleagues and targeted a young Englishman who was newly married and travelling with his American bride. The bridegroom played cards with the three sharps for two nights in his cabin and, on the third evening, the bride spilled her handbag on the deck and a wedding ring rolled out. 'Baldy' Johnson picked up the ring and then noticed that the girl was wearing her own wedding band, and he looked at the band in his hand more closely as the girl explained that she always carried her mother's wedding ring with her. Johnson then returned the ring to the young bride.

During the card game that evening and the next, the luck of the young groom changed and he began to win. Baldy's two confederates thought Baldy was double-crossing them and began to consider taking drastic action against him, but the *Titanic* struck the iceberg before they could do anything. The card game broke up, but the strain of the collision had jammed the door of the cabin closed and trapped the newly-weds with the three sharps. Baldy's confederates began quarrelling over the stateroom's two lifebelts when a revolver appeared in Baldy's hand. The gambler told his friends that the dispute would be settled with the cards and that the first two people being dealt aces would receive the lifebelts. The other sharps assumed Baldy would deal himself an ace and that one of them would receive the other but, to their horror, the bride and groom received both aces. Baldy held his gun ready while his former confederates strapped the lifebelts on the newly-weds, and they then pushed the two young people through a porthole, making it possible for them to be saved (which they were). Their last view of 'Baldy' Johnson revealed him to be sitting at the table, gun close at hand, playing death's head solitaire.

When the girl reached her home in America, she told her mother how 'Baldy' Johnson had saved her life and of the incident on deck where she had dropped her mother's wedding ring. The mother pondered her daughter's story for a while and then went upstairs and came down carrying an old photograph. The daughter looked at it and recognised a young 'Baldy' Johnson. She was then told that the photograph was of the father she had never known, and that Johnson had left her mother right after her birth because he refused to give up gambling.

This romantic legend will serve as an appropriate end to the story of the *Titanic* gamblers. There is a certain fascination with the way of life chosen by these 'gentlemen of the green cloth', and those of the fraternity who survived the sinking of the *Titanic* had a unique chapter written into their life stories when they played a little-known role in one of the great human dramas of history.

APPENDIX 1

'OLD MAN JORDAN'

As we have seen, in 1912 a number of professional gamblers were falsely alleged to have gone down with the *Titanic*. The reader might be interested in learning a bit more about a couple of these men and how they eventually 'cashed in their chips' when their turn to do so finally came to pass.

On 7 September 1918, the following article about 'Old Man Jordan' appeared in the *Oswego Daily Palladium*:

Was Swindler for 50 Years

Baltimore, Md – The death of Jim Jordan at the ripe age of seventy-five years in the Johns Hopkins hospital has brought to an end the career of one of the greatest and most picturesque swindlers that America has ever produced. Jordan was not a 'yeg' or a 'gunman' or a 'holdup man.' He played the confidence game in the early border days, when three-card monte was the center of attractions at the numerous gambling shacks in the West, and later sold 'gold bricks' to the innocent tenderfoots. Toward the end of his career as a confidence man Jordan became a poker shark. He crossed the Atlantic on the luxuriously-equipped liners and never was averse to play a 'quiet little game.' He made a fortune estimated at a million during the half century he operated as a confidence man, but when he died he ran true to form and was broke.

Jordan served his apprenticeship under 'Canada Bill,' the most successful confidence man who roamed the West during the early days. He first was employed as a 'steerer,' but showed such early proficiency that he rapidly came to be full partner to 'Canada Bill.' Jordan soon abandoned the monte game and went into the broader and more lucrative field afforded by the 'gold brick' industry, and rose step by step to be one of the most successful poker sharks that operated on trans-Atlantic liners plying between New York city and European ports.

Jordan had a close call on the ill-fated *Titanic* which was destroyed at sea several years ago. The swindler had been booked for passage and would have sailed had not the steward discovered his identity.

Jim killed two and perhaps three men in the early days of the West. One of his victims was 'Bill' Matthews, killed in Chicago. Jordan made a run for it and reached California, but came back and was picked up by the police in a Chicago cafe. Jim was convicted and sentenced to 20 years in the penitentiary. He served four years when he was pardoned. Jim then joined up with some railroad gamblers and went to Denver, Colo., where he shot Cliff Sparks, an innocent bystander, in a fight in a gambling house. They didn't hang a man in those days for mistakes and Jordan came clear.

In the early border days Jordan's name was known throughout the West. With his partner, 'Canada Bill,' headquarters were established at the famous Marble hall, the rendezvous of 'sports.' They posed as farmers and didn't need any makeup. During the Leadville excitement Jordan and several of his confreres organized a gang that worked the cattle ranch game near Denver, Colo. They secured a small ranch of about forty acres that had a wide range extending into the foothills. In those days there were many Englishmen going to the West looking for ranch investments, and some of these visitors knew very little about Western ways.

Jordan would get in touch with one of these tenderfoots and take him out to his ranch where he would round up a number of cowboys who would reach 'headquarters' just for the fun of trimming their guest. They would have a fake ranch superintendent and a fake set of books showing how many calves they had branded that season. They would point to the wide expanse around their miniature ranch and call it their range. Jordan and his gang probably sold the ranch a dozen times in big figures.

APPENDIX 2

'DOC' OWEN

On 29 December 1907, the *New York Press* published the following article about 'Doc' Owen:

> Some recent writer lamented the fact that piracy is dead and that there is little more of romance or color to tales of the sea. Piracy is not dead; it merely has changed its form. The modern Lafitte does not go to sea in a 'long, low, rakish craft' and flying the Jolly Roger, but here in the stateroom of the most magnificent of sea palaces and armed with a stacked deck of cards. With this deck of cards, he gathers in more plunder year after year than Lafitte, Captain Kidd and the other great adventurers of former time got in their bloody expeditions.

The modern Captain Kidd is the transatlantic card sharper, the man who, traveling as a gentleman, robs every man he can inveigle into a card game for high stakes. There are not too many passenger vessels of the first class that arrive here that do not bring stories of the doings of the pirates: of this man swindled out of money or of that man entering complaint that he lost all his ready cash at play.

The dean of the modern pirate is Jacob, better known as 'Doc' Owen. Aside from the men regularly employed on the liners, he probably is the greatest transatlantic traveler in the world. For the last 15 or 20 years he has crossed the ocean on an average of nearly 40 times a year. He always travels in the best of style. He is a lavish spender, and it is estimated that his expenses rarely fall below $12,000 a year. This figure, no doubt, is modest when it is taken into account that usually he has a confederate whose bills are paid by him. Recently Mr Owen made public announcement of the fact that he had given up the sea, but soon after this declaration came the news of a larger haul by him than any reported for a long time, so his retirement from the game did not last.

The 'Doc' is middle-aged, rather above than below the average height, with keen eyes, pockmarked face, a large mouth, with thick lips which droop at the corners, and a scar on the back of his left hand. His manners are ingratiating and his speech is that of one who is neither ignorant nor especially well-educated, but certainly well-informed. And his skill at cards is certainly great, though his victim will not claim to have detected him in anything positively crooked. For it is not of record that he has been actually engaged in any net which in former times would have been held to justify shooting. And further than this, the passengers on the steamships would not and could not testify from personal knowledge.

Dukes, Earls, Lords, Counts, Barons, princes of finance and plain, ordinary men of money have been the victims of 'Doc' and his confederates. If his expenses in the 15 or 20 years he has been crossing the sea have aggregated approximately $200,000, it is reasonable to estimate that his winnings, or rather his stealings, have been from $300,000 to $500,000. Of course, a fair proportion of his winnings go to those who make it possible for him to continue his fleecing operations despite the great amount of notoriety that has attended some of his exploits.

Usually 'Doc' is not in port more than twenty-four hours. Sometimes he is in New York only a few hours. Immediately on the arrival of one liner he hurries to the pier of another company to catch an outgoing vessel, and when that one arrives at Queenstown, Cherbourg or Southampton he races to catch the first vessel returning. The 'Doc' certainly is industrious. He is well advised of the doings of rich men of sporting inclinations, such as John W. Gates and Charles M. Schwab, and if they want 'action' while crossing the ocean the 'Doc' usually is on hand to accommodate them. But the men who suffer most from 'Doc' Owen and his kind are those to whom the loss of $500 or $1,000 or $1,500 is a tragedy. If half the stories that are known by the foreign Consuls in New York about 'Doc' Owen and his pals were to be told, a little light would be cast on the darkest side of the modern pirates' game.

It might be supposed that the officials of the great transatlantic lines would know something of a man who crosses the ocean 40 times a year, spending money lavishly and playing cards every time he finds a chance to play for important money. What they might be supposed to know, however, bears no close resemblance to what they have to say. They will repeat a description of the man like that just given and will earnestly protest that they try to protect their passengers from the wiles and devices of 'Doc' Owen and other like pirates. They declare almost plaintively that they are unable to prevent gamblers like him from traveling on their ships. And then they will tell, with elaborate details, of the various precautions that are taken by the captains of the ships to prevent their unsuspecting passengers from being victimized.

Ask a sporting man, as gamblers euphemistically call themselves, what he knows of 'Doc' Owen, and he will answer, as one of the best known of the ilk did this week:

'Doc Owen? Oh, yes, I know Doc. He's a tip-top poker player. Never heard of him playing bank. Poker's his specialty. Ocean steamers? Yes, he's been working the ships quite a few years now. Pretty lucky at it, too, I reckon. Anyhow, he keeps traveling most of the time. Where did he come from, and who is he? Well, say. Look out there on Broadway and watch the crowd. Inside of 20 minutes you'll see a hundred men passing that you and I know and most everybody on the Great White Way knows. How many of them can you tell about? We don't know who they are or where they come from. Nor we don't care. They just showed up in New York and made good. That's all there is to them, and that's all there is to Doc Owen.'

Those who ought to know say that 'Doc' Owen has the same working arrangement with steamship officers that poolroom keepers and faro bank owners have with the police. He gets 'protection' so far as they can give it, just as the city gamblers get protection so far as the police can give it. What is not quite clear is that the company officials and the agents of the line do not put an end to this illicit traffic. Of course, 'Doc' Owen and all the gamblers who 'work' the boats are as well-known to the detectives assigned to the transatlantic piers as are the captains of the various vessels, and they could arrest Owen and his kind as suspicious characters every time they appear, but they do not do it, and apparently have no desire to interfere so long as the steamship people are content to let the gamblers travel without molestation.

One thing that can be said in favor of Owen is that he plays no favorites. A few years ago one of 'Larry' Summerfield's numerous flirtations with the criminal law of whatever country he happened to be in landed him in a prison in Paris, with an excellent prospect of prolonging his stay behind bars for a protracted period, and, as his custom was, he appealed to his pals for assistance.

Such appeals are seldom made in vain, and in this instance Chappy Moran, who was perhaps the nearest to Summerfield of any man in his line of business, responded manfully. He started immediately for France, taking with him a well-known lawyer of this city, whose success in criminal cases had earned him a reputation.

After completing his business in Paris, the lawyer started at once for home, and on his first appearance on the deck of the steamer he came on he was accosted by a pleasant-spoken man, who called him by name and professed great pleasure in meeting him.

'I imagine you must know me,' he said, 'for I am pretty well-known in New York. I'm Dr. Owen. If you don't know me personally you must know my Optical Goods establishment on Forty-second Street.'

The effrontery of using his own name and introducing himself to a New York criminal lawyer seems almost beyond belief, but he carried his point, and established an intimacy which not unnaturally let up to a 'friendly' game of cards in the smoking room. And this the lawyer found expensive.

After the lawyer reached home he learned who 'Doc' Owen really was, and feeling more than a little sore he sought the gambler out and remonstrated with him. 'I don't think it's fair,' he said, 'for you to "trim" me the way you did when I was just returning from a trip I took to serve one of your friends. I did all I could for him, and was entitled to some consideration on your part. I think you ought to give me back that $300.'

'Well,' said Owen, 'I'll tell you what I'll do. You get my picture out of the rogues' gallery and I'll give you the $300.' So the lawyer tried and was unsuccessful.

'Doc' is married and has his home in this city. When he is here, he manages to keep out of notice generally, but has made several attempts to establish poker games here. It appears, however, that he is not diplomatic enough to succeed in avoiding police interference, for his games have been given up, for some reason, while numberless others have continued, and he has each time returned to his travel on the steamships. In this he is easily the most successful of the many gamblers who have undertaken the fleecing of ocean travelers.

Concerning his success at play there is no mystery whatever. The warmest admirer of Doc Owen, if it be conceded that he has admirers, would never pretend that he played a square game of poker. He is called one of the most skillful manipulators of cards who make a living out of crooked play, and there was probably no single device of the illegitimate game that is not at his fingers' ends. More than that, he usually, or at least very frequently, has a confederate in the game with him, and no man who plays poker need to be told what enormous advantages can be taken by two who play together against the others in the game.

For such operations as his there is no more fruitful field than the smoking room of an ocean liner. The passengers are nearly all men of affairs, to say the least, to whom some sort of occupation or excitement is almost a necessity, and since there is really little to do on board ship they gravitate naturally to the smoking room. A game of cards is the most attractive excitement available, and they sit in with perhaps no intention of playing heavily. The rest is easy.

There are two beliefs that dwell in the minds of most men that aid swindlers like Owen. One is the notion the average smoking room frequenter has in his own abilities as a poker player, and the other is his blind faith in his own luck. It is on these convictions that 'Doc' trades and rakes in his money. He knows that each man starts into the game in the firm belief that he is going to win out, and once the excitement of the game has reached his brain 'Doc' knows how to bait him along, feeding him a small jackpot occasionally, to keep him encouraged, till finally the fatuous man has put in his last penny and is cleaned out. There is scarcely a liner on which the 'Doc' has been a passenger that does not regularly discharge at the end of its trip one or more passengers 'stone-broke.'

On 11 February 1922 the following article about 'Doc' Owen appeared in the Fairmont *West Virginian*:

New York, February 11 – News reached New York today of the death at Havana on January 14 of W.J. (Doc.) Owens, a notorious old-time gambler, considered one of the most expert card men of his time. He fell down stairs at a hotel and died soon afterwards.

Gamblers here say his equal never lived. He operated mainly on trans-Atlantic liners until the steamship companies barred him from sailing. In 1906 he was reported to have won $200,000 from William Thaw of Pittsburgh, although both denied the story.

When he arrived on the steamer *Majestic* from England in 1905, the passengers presented him with a loving cup for refraining from card playing during the voyage. He broke into the headlines at the time of the *Titanic* disaster when it was reported in the press on both sides of the ocean that he had escaped in a life boat by disguising himself as a woman. He denied the report and said he would bring suit for libel, but he never did.

APPENDIX 3

HARRY SILBERBERG

On 16 August 1903 the *New York Herald* published a lengthy first-hand interview with grifter Harry Silberberg, who was briefly rumoured to have gone down with the *Titanic*. Although we have given a very brief outline of Silberberg's life earlier in this book, the present first-hand interview gives such an accurate description of the mentality of a typical early twentieth-century con man that we are presenting the entire interview here for the reader's consideration. (Note: despite Silberberg's stated intention in 1903 to go straight, he was still pulling con games on innocent victims as late as the early 1920s.)

At last the identity and mystery of 'J. Coleman Drayton,' the impersonator of the well-known New York millionaire, is solved. The young man says he has come to New York to turn over a new leaf. He registers under another name. He will tell the story of his adventures in a book, and as a preliminary act of confession he gives the *Herald* the leading episodes in his astounding career. He is without doubt the most consummate all-round sharper and trickster in the world.

It is a remarkable narrative, and concerns his life from the time he became a clerk in his father's store, in a little frontier town, until he travelled over Europe with an Austrian Countess, duping tradesmen and squandering fortunes in a series of luxurious revels.

Speaking five languages; occasionally going to jail, getting out again; returning to America and marrying several women – heiresses and widows – and keeping an establishment with an adventuress; obtaining large sums of money under the name of J.C. Drayton; again to be arrested, but always escaping, he seemingly led a sort of charmed life.

In his confession to the *Herald* he says that he began by studying law enough to escape technical violations, also reading up the international statutes and carefully planning his financial adventures to escape severe punishment.

The newspapers of America and Europe have teemed with accounts of his operations. Through an error, a lot of his photographs were forwarded from Budapest to the real J. Coleman Drayton, at the Langham Hotel, London. These Mr. Drayton gave to Robert Pinkerton, with instructions to hunt the impostor down and bring him to justice. He says, by the way, that five thousand of these photographs were made and distributed among the police of America and Europe. His description and record are on file with police headquarters in every important city in the world. It was a great scene in Chicago when the impostor was confronted by the real Mr. Drayton in the Auditorium Hotel. Mr. Pinkerton had telegraphed the New York banker to hurry on to meet the man. But the spurious Drayton was nowise nonplussed. With a lady on his arm he greeted Mr. Drayton and assured him he had a right to the name 'J.C. Drayton.'

Despite all this, the counterfeit Mr. Drayton now comes forward and confesses to the *Herald*. He hopes it will be a warning to fast young men and women against dishonesty, gambling, dissipation and unscrupulous women. 'There is something back of my life,' said the young man last evening, 'some influence that I never could explain. Some strange psychological power controls me. What it is, science alone can tell. I only know that I have done a thousand strange things against my better judgment – against my will. I must have been a fool, for there is no escape for a man who does wrong. It is only a question of time when Nemesis will overtake him.

'I have found, in every instance, that the women on whom I squandered thousands, whether as companions or my wedded wives, have accepted me in a spirit of adventure. I ultimately discovered that supposed respectable women had secretly gone more or less astray, and had thought to dupe me, only to find themselves united to a man of false names, and obtaining money dishonestly.

'Somewhere in my ancestry there must have been dark blood. Someone must have been bad or I would not have this temperament of evil. My mother was a fine woman, a Pole, full of nobility and honorable sentiments. My father was a good man, industrious and square dealing.

'The key to my evil success, if it may be called such, has been my personality and lavishness with money, attracting gamblers who sought to use me as a decoy. In nearly every Western town I knew the prominent men. When they came to New York, it was easy to use them to my financial advantage, and at the same time to hold my own against the gamblers who wanted them to spend money in their establishments.

'How easy it seems when the game is properly worked. I managed it in this way: – I tell the proprietor of a big Fifth Avenue restaurant that I wish to give a little dinner to a few friends. As he does not know me, I place $500 with him to my credit. This is repeated at one or two large hotels, theatres and other places. The dinner over, I sign the check and tell the waiter to charge it. I send my friends to the theatre with a box at their disposal. I take them to a jewelry store for scarf pins or some pretty tokens, and let them hear me say "Please charge it to my account".

'This gives me standing among the Western men. I have a lot of them at my fingers' ends, and it becomes easy to take them around to Canfield's and other big gambling establishments, for which the gamblers pay me handsomely. Of course, I gamble myself and lose money with the rest, otherwise I would be worth a fortune to-day.'

Such are a few introductory touches regarding the methods of the spurious J. Cole Drayton, Esquire.

'My real name is Harry Silberberg. My father, William Silberberg, was a Jewish rabbi, a man of great gifts, with a genius for public speaking. He came here from Warsaw, Poland, a young man of twenty-six, and married a beautiful young Polish woman in Milwaukee. He had a synagogue in Memphis, Tenn., but later drifted into business and became a merchant. In the civil war he turned blockade runner and made a fortune. When peace was declared, he went to Chicago and was associated with Francis Peabody in real estate, until a turn of fortune left him bankrupt. In 1870 he opened a store at Atlanta, Ga., having credit with H.B. Claflin & Co. Again, he failed. In Atlanta I was born, the youngest of nine children – six now dead. My oldest sister is the richest woman in a town of Arkansas, where our family has remained since my father's death.'

The young man relates how his father made a fortune at Fort Smith out of Indian contracts. He represented the pool interested in the settlement of the Choctaw claims. The government paid $20,000,000 to square the claim of a group of Indians for lands opened to settlers. After the boy had received a common school education at Fort Smith his father died, leaving a chain of stores in Kansas, Arkansas and Missouri. He was but fifteen, and his brother Aaron only twenty-one, but being the only male members of the family, they took charge of the stores. In four years, with new blood, their business had extended until they had twelve stores in different states.

'This wonderful success was the beginning of my downfall. I made money so easily that I spent it recklessly, and I became the talk of the country. Gamblers flocked in to see the gayest young man of the State squandering thousands on women, wine and cards. Gamblers not only came from Kansas City, St. Louis and California to get my money, but they brought pretty girls with them.

'Result – I lost heavily and in five months spent the larger part of the revenue of the six stores I was running in what was called the Kansas and Missouri circuit. My brother ran the Arkansas and Indian Territory stores.

'When he took charge and went over my books he found I was $87,000 short. His severity touched my boyish pride, and like a fool I went to California, leaving a great business behind; I secured a job as advertisement writer and easily made $100 a week in fees from the merchants and commissions from the newspapers. But I was soon in debt. Up to this date I had squandered no money not our own. Mother sent me funds in emergencies, tens of thousands of dollars. Had I worked as hard and shown as much ingenuity in building up the business my father left as I have in devising new methods of rascality, I would be worth millions today.

'My San Francisco fiasco occurred in 1891, and as everybody had the Mexican fever I followed "Jack" Follansbee and some California millionaires to Chihuahua, where everything was booming. My money soon vanished and I hit upon a plan to get more. A Chihuahua telegraph operator told me of the big fortunes weekly transmitted by wire from the States. He said that one [Mr] Goodman had received $50,000, telegraphed him from the Boatmen's Bank in St. Louis.

'Instantly I saw my chance. I consulted the operator and arranged a deal. He agreed to help me out for one-half the proceeds. Then I called on the McMannus Brothers, of the Commercial Bank of Chihuahua, and said I had money on deposit in St. Louis and wanted to get it. I was informed that I would have to have it telegraphed through the Boatmen's Bank. That concern was their agent, and they had a code by which their money was sent.

'It took the operator a few minutes to write a fictitious dispatch and put on all the official earmarks of a genuine message. It purported to be from the Boatmen's Bank in St. Louis, saying that I had deposited $50,000 there. On showing this dispatch I received that amount from the Chihuahua Bank. The truth is that McMannus Co. were anxious to transfer money by wire – it was immensely profitable. They should have made about $4,500 in exchange on that one transaction.

'I gave the operator 25,000 Mexican dollars net, and, like a fool, he instantly locked up his office at midday and took to the wilderness, leaving the country on foot, when he had fully five days' time to get away before the St. Louis bank could be heard from by mail. He should have closed his office later at night. I took the train that evening for El Paso.

'McMannus, however, happening to have a telegram to send and finding the office closed, concluded something was wrong. After waiting five hours he notified the police and ordered my arrest. I was overhauled on the train half-way to El Paso, taken back and kept in a horrible dungeon for five weeks. It was impossible for me to communicate with anyone. The Mexican law decrees that a culprit must be cut off from the world to prevent false testimony or his getting influence to his aid.

'Fortunately, during the next three weeks the news reached my home and the Fort Smith papers published the whole story.

My mother secured strong letters from the Governor of Arkansas and the Supreme Court Judge of the State, who had known me from infancy. She also had the necessary money to repay the bank the $25,000 taken by the operator and the $1,000 I had used of the money in paying my debts. The operator, by the way, is still a fugitive and has never been heard from. The case was finally settled and I was sentenced to three years' imprisonment.

'Later, because of my youth and the refunding of the money by my mother, together with the personal appeals from officials in Arkansas, I was paroled in the custody of the Governor of Chihuahua, Miguel Ahumada, whose secretary I became through knowing how to use the American typewriter. In this capacity I served nine months, when, through petitions from leading men of Arkansas, I was pardoned in the latter part of 1892. I took the train direct for New York, and to this day have never returned to Fort Smith.

'I reached New York with about $500 in my pocket, but I had enough experience and knowledge to fill a house. During my nine months as secretary to the Governor there was little to do, so I studied for all I was worth. I studied day and night to rid myself of certain mispronunciations and mistakes in the English grammar. I also mastered Spanish, already knowing Polish, besides getting a fair smattering of French, solely by my own efforts in studying from books. Later I studied etiquette and prepared myself for a wider field abroad.

'In New York I found employment again in writing advertisements and reading matter notices for business firms, and became expert at the business. I determined to make money honestly and lead a proper life. I published a guide for shoppers, opening an office in one of the Broadway skyscrapers and taking rooms in an uptown hotel.

'But, alas, with money the devil returned in the shape of evil influences, and I was to soon playing the races and in debt up to my neck. Like a coward I went to Baltimore to escape paying my debts, met the proprietor of a leading Baltimore paper and posed under the name of Whitney. He took a fancy to me and gave me a chance to write advertisements. I prospered and lived at the Rennert Hotel.

'A convention of architects was held there about that time, and a Chicago firm gave me $3,000 to get it a contract for building certain important structures. I was wrong in accepting the money, for I had no influence and failed to secure the contract. But the $3,000 put me on my feet in fine shape.

'Next I turned up in Rochester, N.Y., under the name of J.C. Davis, made the acquaintance of a rich and beautiful widow, the daughter of a lumber millionaire, and married her. I was then twenty-five years old and in the best of spirits and felt that I could meet any emergency in life. She had been divorced from her husband, a doctor, and was not allowed to marry in New York. We chartered a special car and went to Canada for the ceremony. There were forty guests with champagne and much gayety. We were married at St. Catharine's, thence going to California on our bridal trip, stopping at the principal points en route.

'I thought I was in clover, for the widow had a private income of $25,000 per year, but I did not realize that her property was tied up by a wise provision, so that not a cent of it could be squandered. In St. Paul I lost several thousand dollars gambling, and reached San Francisco again a bankrupt.

'However, the pretty young widow, now my wife, was cheerful, and I proceeded to manufacture, by the aid of a lithographer, exchange drafts, which were made out in proper form. I secured money on these drafts to the amount of about four thousand six hundred dollars. Result – we were arrested – she as my accomplice – and thrown into jail. Her father came to the rescue and we finally got free. That was a tough experience for a newly married man on his wedding tour, but the jail feature did not please my wife. She secured a divorce.

'This was in 1895. From California I went to Europe by way of Vera Cruz [Veracruz] and Havana, landed in Spain, did Monte Carlo,

Rome, Venice and other cities and finally turned up in Berlin, where I met Mr. Louis Langerman, representing an American corporation and now US Consul to Morocco. He was destined to play an important part in my life.

'It came about in this way. He invited me to visit him at Vienna. We lived at the Hotel Imperial and patronized the races. An event occurred that proved my undoing. One evening at a grand miniature Venice spectacle, five times larger than the Madison Square Garden, and one of the sights of the city, I took a ride in a gondola on the artificial canal. The boat was genuinely Italian. Only two or three persons besides myself were in the gondola when a lady of unusual beauty entered. She was a Countess, accompanied by her husband, in full Austrian regimentals.

'I had recently been in Venice and knew the Italian custom of rising when a lady entered a gondola. I did so and observed that the lady seemed attracted by the act, as none of the others arose.

'I did not then know that she was a Venetian by birth. A few days later she saw me riding on the Prado behind a team of Russian racing horses. I was with Langerman, whom the Countess knew, and she recognized me as the man of the gondola. Langerman was invited to present me, and I met the Countess. To say that I was charmed with her witchery, beauty and chic but faintly expresses the impression she made, and it was the beginning of a long romance. The presentation launched me at once into the exclusive social world of Vienna. Our acquaintance ripened, and she introduced me to some of the first families of Europe. Invitations to functions and entertainments followed, and I had to make returns which rapidly reduced my funds.

'We became intimate and she secured a divorce from her husband, keeping one of the children. Then we were openly together. Like all Europeans of a certain class, even the highest circles, the lady in the case wanted money and believed the American purse inexhaustible. I had spent my funds giving her handsome presents, in entertaining

189

and, in fact, conveying the impression that I was of bonanza wealth, so she could not be blamed for anticipating endless fortune and luxury on the part of a prodigal foreigner.

'But my end was in sight, and there was nothing but to tell her frankly my circumstances or retire. The truth is, I was rather glad of a chance to tell her. I said I was bankrupt. She was astonished, couldn't and wouldn't believe it until a week had passed and I announced I would have to leave her, having reached the end of my resources.

'Then the Countess showed me that she was not a mercenary woman of the hour, but my friend. She was equal to the situation, and decided what should be done. I was travelling under my own name. She said she had looked it up through the embassy and found it lacked prominence. She added, "There is a name well known in Europe allied with a very great family – the Astors. You take that name. Call yourself J.C. Drayton and I will secure you unlimited credit."

'Being deeply smitten with the Countess, fond of adventure and short of cash, it took me but a moment to decide. We arranged a programme of action. I ordered cards and stationery engraved J. Cunningham Drayton, and had the name put on my luggage. Then we left for Baden Baden.

'In that city the Countess, who knew everybody, presented me right and left. To each introduction she added in a whisper, "He is of the Astors." That put me in exclusive circles. The Baden Baden papers announced my arrival and chronicled daily coaching parades, which attracted attention. Being a fair whip, I was at home with horses.

'It was said I was in love with the Countess and squandering a fortune on her, so everybody was glad to see me. It prepared the way for raising money. The Countess visited the diamond shops and confirmed the rumor that I was to make her handsome presents which she was there to select.

'My purchases amounted to 40,000 marks. The gems were charged to my account and the merchants were disappointed that I did not buy more. I did not intend to defraud the shopkeepers, but use them temporarily, for I had bigger game in view and made my purchases modest on purpose. The bigger game was a party of six or seven millionaires interested in the Countess. She was a wonder in fascinating men, especially rich Americans.

'They invited us on a trip to Carlsbad, and knowing that they were heavy gamblers I hoped to win a lot of money at baccarat. I had learned card playing among the poker sharps of the frontier. Unfortunately, two a of the party met a Hungarian prince, who was attentive to a Philadelphia heiress and was anxious to secure their friendship. He gave them entertainments and horseback trips into the mountains of a most romantic character. Result, everybody was too tired for cards in the evening. When the party separated, we went to England for cash and more adventures.

'I had previously met Mr. Louis Palmer, of the great biscuit firm of Huntly & Palmer, and I thought I would accept his invitation to visit him, thus opening the way to getting more money.

'In London we occupied five rooms at the Hotel Cecil, lived in luxury and were having a fine time with noted people when the blow fell. An extradition warrant caused my arrest for the Baden Baden diamond transaction.

'It was consolation to find the Countess true. She visited me in prison and offered to settle for the diamonds, but the case had gone too far. Once in a German court, proceedings cannot be settled – the law must take its course.

'My arrest came about in this way. The real J.C. Drayton happened to be at the Langham in London, with his name announced in the papers, which caused my photographer in Budapest to send him a lot of pictures I had ordered. I was at the Victoria. Of course, the real Drayton got them, and thus was able to give Scotland Yard detectives the pictures and evidence they had long needed to establish my identity, and make a strong case.

'I was taken to Germany and sentenced to three years by a court of five judges. In the excitement of the affair, without a chance to meet the changes of weather with proper clothing I caught cold, had pleurisy and was near death. Home friends through our representatives in Congress and the American Consul, Mr. Theriot, at Manheim, obtained my pardon. After serving a few months I was given a sort of ticket of leave, escorted to Bremen, put aboard a steamer and sent with other criminals to America, German style.

'Meanwhile, the Countess was in Paris leading an adventurous life. Meeting government officials and military officers she became possessed of their secret, which was the beginning of the conspiracy to convict Dreyfus. She became the famous woman in the Dreyfus case, and made a fortune by selling these secrets backward and forward during that terrible episode.

'Two years ago I saw the Countess in Paris. She was as radiant as ever, yet a changed woman. People have wondered why she was able to figure so much in the Dreyfus affair. She was a woman of extraordinary resources, one of the most fascinating, brilliant, intellectual and really wonderful women I ever heard of, a tall, distinguished, high bred Venetian, possessed of all the arts and graces of the women of the Italian court. Such is she whom I met in the gondola.

'Next the scene changes to America. In the year 1897 I visited Texas for my health, because of the chest trouble contracted in Germany. I intended to change my name, but in Baltimore en route I met a lovely Maryland girl who had known me as Drayton in Europe, and she addressed me by that name in Baltimore. I kept up the deception, and was surprised that she had not heard of the Baden Baden scandal and my arrest. After a short flirtation I went to Dallas, Texas, and almost immediately married the rich Clara B., as was published in the *Herald* at that time.

'I was now about thirty years old and thought it was time to reform. I realized I was on the wrong track, so I went to Denver and resumed special advertising and "write-ups." In the interest of the proprietor of a Denver journal I began exposés of certain mining frauds which netted large sums of money. Some weeks my share amounted to $300 and more. After my European experience I was able to entertain handsomely and get into Rocky Mountain society – some social peaks higher than others.

'I was still Drayton, but passed as a cousin and not the real J. Coleman Drayton. A political campaign was on and I made public speeches, having inherited gifts from my father for oratory. My address at Colorado Springs caused Governor Thomas to appoint me commissioner to raise funds for a special mining exhibit at the Paris Exposition. I was successful in getting handsome subscriptions, but none reached Paris.

'During my tour through the mining districts I had a private car and spent $35,000 for entertainments. The Governor was a democrat, and the republican press fought me so bitterly that I resigned and went to Montana.

'There I entered the service of Senator William A. Clark, who was seeking re-election. Being a successful public speaker and knowing how to win votes, I succeeded from the start. The Senator's son, Charles, I liked immensely and persuaded him to invest in newspapers. Five newspapers were acquired outright. My share was an appointment as editor of the *Great Falls Tribune*. My salary was $600 a month – $300 from the paper and $300 from the Senator's son.

'This was an event in my life, and I might at have made it a stepping stone to honorable achievement. It was the one opportunity of a career. Every favor was showered on me and I had things my own way until an expert went over the books and reported me too extravagant even for Montana and Colorado financial roundup.

'I took rooms at the Waldorf and cut a wide swath. It was easy to arrange a plan of campaign, for I knew the principal men of the West. I contracted with certain gambling houses to introduce Westerners. In bringing this about I gave sumptuous dinners and made a great impression on visiting miners and cattle kings.

'During this New York experience I squandered about one hundred thousand dollars – most of it went for entertainments and the races. While I worked for gamblers and entertained actresses and men about town, I met another brilliant woman, well-known in New York. I told a certain Broadway theatre proprietor, who was running a vaudeville house, paying his girls little or no salary and receiving large sums from rich men for bringing about desired introductions, that I did not think much of his women. He seemed annoyed, for, thinking me rich, he kept his eye on me as a good one to bleed.

'One day his agent, acting as intermediary between the theatre and rich men about town, Wall Street brokers and patrons of gambling houses, said to me: – "Don't imagine that our actresses are the only beauties at our command. If you really want to meet a stunning woman of refinement and society connection, I can accommodate you." So he introduced me to Mrs. Susette, a fine-looking lady of charming, companionable manners. We became attached from the start, and sailed for Europe, on the *St. Louis*, on July 18, 1901. In Paris we planned a trip around the world, and sailed from Genoa in October of that year. This lady believed me the genuine Drayton, and on a promise of marriage consented to make the tour.

'As "Mrs. Drayton" she was a valuable ally in all my plans, though innocent of my identity. Her fine presence and pleasing personality won powerful friends. The part in this trip that became famous was our meeting at Port Said with Sir John Ridgeway, Governor of Ceylon, and "Tom" Walker, a millionaire Scotchman of the island. As I was travelling with a retinue of servants, fine dogs and every evidence of wealth, we were royally welcomed everywhere.

'When Millionaire Walker suggested that I buy his horses at Calcutta and race them during the Viceroy meet I concurred and gave him my I.O.U. for 16,000 rupees, promising to stop over at Calcutta and do the races. I carried strong letters from the Governor and Mr. Walker, and going to that city as an owner of horses, and bearing the name of Drayton, I had things my own way.

'I was put up at the clubs, invited to the swell functions and enabled to bet in any amount on credit. This I did to the extent of more than 200,000 rupees – about $66,000 – which amount, by the way, I still owe the Calcutta bookies. For once I had an even "break".

'My departure from Calcutta was due to the fact that I did not want to expose my hand, for I had deposited bogus drafts to the amount of $50,000 and told the bookmakers that it would cover my losses. As there is no law to collect gambling debts, I could not be held for the offence.

'We made a triumphal tour through India, stopping at the noted places, and finally reached Japan. Arriving at Tokio, I presented Minister Buck my credentials – which I had carefully manufactured – to the effect that I was empowered to act as a member of the firm of Drayton, Endicott & Co., a bogus firm, of course. The scheme worked to a charm. I was placed on strong footing at the embassy, received courtesies, special privileges at state functions, such as the cherry blossom fêtes at the temple city of Kioto [Kyoto] and at the lawn party of the Mikado; also, a number of dinners.

'"Mrs. Drayton" impressed people and was of great service to me in matters of society etiquette, which, with our abundant means, gave us standing, and I don't think our identity was ever questioned. We stopped five weeks in the Philippines, where I promoted several schemes. I bought a bankrupt bus line in Australia for Philippine service and established a rikshaw company.

'In Siam I was entertained by the King on presenting the credentials which I had manufactured and plastered with ribbons and great seals. I informed His Majesty that I wanted to build an American rail-road in Siam. At the conclusion of a royal banquet of many courses, with especial attentions showered on the King by "Mrs. Drayton", I received a valuable railroad concession through the famous teakwood country. The line was to be thirty-six miles long and the concession good for ninety-nine years. I have it yet, and but for the Pinkertons I might have made a fortune out of the railroad.

'In India we were entertained by the Viceroy, Lord Curzon, and his wife, invited to a state banquet, and at the races we sat in the royal box. I posed simply as J. Cunningham Drayton and expressed my disapproval of the real Mr. Drayton's marriage, and at times criticized him severely. This made an impression and established my standing beyond question. I had previously met Mrs. Arthur Paget and won her good graces, which enabled me to meet many great people. Thus it was that I reached the Viceroy and his charming Chicago wife.'

Such are some of the adventures of this thrifty young graduate of the mercantile post trading schools of the Indian Territory country. A strange feature of his career is that in the face of ninety-seven newspapers exposing his identity last July, with Pinkerton's circulars sent broadcast with his photograph, he was enabled to marry two wealthy and prominent women in Texas – a widow of El Paso, who gave him $20,000 outright, he says, and another lady, of Houston. Each was worth $200,000. With the $20,000 from his bride redeemed Mrs. 'Drayton's' diamonds from pawnbrokers in London. The Texas police did not discover his identity in these marriages until too late. Both victims were granted quick divorces to protect their property from the alleged Drayton. The El Paso lady was granted a divorce in three hours, and the Houston lady in two days.

Perhaps nothing has played a more curious part in the young man's operations than a certain French bulldog. Of it he says:

'I bought the dog in Paris, of the Chien de Luxe Kennels, for 5,000 francs. It proved a most valuable aid in giving me a speedy acquaintance with prominent people whom I wished to know, especially women. Anyone seeing a dog like my French bull would naturally admire it. It opened the way to further acquaintance – one word leads to another.

'I knew this weakness of human nature and bought the dog expressly to extend my acquaintance with men and women of money. I had only to parade the animal in the way of these people, and they were sure to inquire about the dog, and when they found that I was the famous J.C. Drayton, the New York millionaire and society man, allied to the Astors by marriage, all the rest was easy.

'There is nothing like a stunning dog to open the way to a pretty woman's heart. My dog was finally stolen from me at the Auditorium in Chicago. A detective, on my trail with a dozen others, captured the dog one day. I accused him and threatened proceedings. He said he knew nothing about the dog, and advised me to keep still, as he could be of value to me. In the end I learned what the detectives were doing, how much they were paid by the agency, and how much Mr. Drayton was charged for keeping me under surveillance. I have nothing to fear.

'As I have said, I studied law enough to know within what limits I could act. There is nothing about my recent operations here or in Europe to make me serious trouble. At the same time, I see how wrong my course has been. It is time to turn over a new leaf. I prefer to tell my own story, and leave the police to make the best of it. I have been married four times, but divorced in each case, and in two instances given the quickest divorce on record in any State.'

A strong point with the young adventurer is his simple, straightforward, unassuming manner – frank, fair and pleasing. Every word he utters seems the truth. He appears not more than twenty-five or twenty-six, yet he is thirty-three. He looks like a college young man, or a military cadet, tall, lithe in form, slender, muscular and always self-possessed.

He has dark brown eyes and dark hair. He looks and talks like a well-educated, well-mannered and properly conducted American young man of good family. In conversation he makes no mistakes in grammar and pronunciation; never becomes excited or loses his temper. In a word, he is a self-possessed, fascinating young man, who knows the world and many of the noted people in it.

APPENDIX 4

'BUD' HAUSER

At the beginning of this book we discussed gambler 'Bud' Hauser and the way he met his death on the *Olympic* in April 1912. On 2 June 1912 *The Washington Post* published the following article about Hauser and the shady way he made his living:

> They went through a small formality in New York headquarters the other day. They opened the safe in which department records are kept, and, following the law, removed therefrom one 'Bud' Hauser, cardsharp and several and-so-forths.

The police have much on him, for he, for the most part, operated outside the three-mile limit and his victims, for the most part, kept their troubles to themselves. But 'Bud' Hauser was a terror of the deep. He lived the clawhammer kind of life, making of the dress suit the raiment of roguery. He turned the trick card sailing East and threw the trained dice sailing west.

He was college bred. He was a traveler. He followed the insecure bank roll up the green Nile, pursued it at Nice, played it in Paris or trailed it to Berlin. But it was on the transatlantic liners that he operated most. He gambled and won whenever it was necessary. Aces were his latitude, deuces has longitude, nerve his barometer.

He died appropriately in a ship's cabin with a fresh-won stake in his hand.

Speaking of 'Bud' Hauser, you wouldn't go wrong if you called him an eel, for he was as slippery as they make 'em, and couldn't he wriggle! And calling him a shark wouldn't hit wide of the mark, for he was a terror of the deep and not over-particular what came to his maw; besides, a pilot fish in petticoats was as like as not to be with him for such advice as sharks most require.

'Bud' Hauser – a versatile person, player of cards, thrower of trained dice, transatlantic and shore sharper, and withal, a man of force, education and wide travel, who fitted in a drawing room and never felt ill at ease at a salon. It was once said of him in a way intended to be complimentary, that, whenever or wherever confidence was misplaced, if 'Bud' was around he usually had it. He lived that way, and he lived well.

New York was his home port. Between sailings he kept largely in the white light. He shuttled between the foyers of the great hotels and the rendezvous of the underworld. Wealth and respectability, not knowing, gave him its hand. In the all-night restaurant he had a special table. His car was always waiting. He was a first-nighter at the opera. At times the pilot fish was with him, reserved, polite.

He seldom disturbed the police, as they seldom disturbed him. Thus he lived ashore, looking always the Doctor Jekyll, having little use for the mask of Mr Hyde.

'Bud' Houser came into the world honest enough, and keeping straight was natural with him until he had read sophomore economics at Columbia and hit out for the West. There he sought to apply the principles of Adam Smith to certain running races at seven furlongs, but the principles didn't apply. Resourceful, he turned to trickery, and as the game of chance is played he had what is termed the edge on the other fellow and won. From that time on his art or profession, whichever way you like it best, was to get between a man and his bankroll.

A gambler of promise and performance, one 'Lucky' Baldwin of the Pacific coast accepted the Hauser talents at their face value. Baldwin owned a stable which in the days of ponies and poolrooms was a large money getter. 'Bud' Hauser became a betting commissioner for said Baldwin, following the stable and the bankroll wherever the bookmakers noted the improvement in the breed of horses on their betting sheets.

At the racetrack one day 'Bud' Hauser met 'Doc' Owen, who had been known for a number of years as the ideal knight of the green cloth on the deep-sea going ships and by the shorter title of 'boob catcher.' 'Doc' Owen was temporarily sojourning ashore. He had ample funds. Pride of achievement had made him garrulous, and he told Hauser that on his last trip from Europe, at about eight bells, he had been lucky enough to retire from a card game with $20,000 and a reputation. 'Bud' Hauser immediately had an attack of the sea fidgets. Why putter ashore with chances like that showing all the way from Fire Island to Land's End?

An incident not infrequently changes the entire course of a man's life. 'Doc' Owen was an incident to 'Bud' Hauser. At the next Saturday sailing Hauser was a passenger on a French liner, having a stateroom between a theologian and the over-rich son of a pioneer in the byproducts of petroleum. He never once disturbed the theologian.

Hauser emulated Owen. He had learned the crooked niceties of cards as an incident to horse racing; he had picked up the tricks of rolling dice so that they would first tantalize and then triumph. He had the neatness and dispatch of 'Big Bill' McCrey, the assurance and boldness of 'Colonel' Torrey and the bonhomie of 'Doc' Owen. They were mere soldiers, or, better still, sailors of fortune. He became a captain.

The day that 'Doc' Owen made the fatal faux pas of uncovering the fifth queen in a strongly stimulated poker game 30 knots east of Nantucket 'Bud' Hauser saw his own great opportunity. He became the recognized head of the gamblers on shipboard, and he held the post against all comers until he drew the six spades which, among gamblers, means never again.

By measurements and markings known alike to the police and travellers, 'Bud' Hauser was tall, slim, scarred on one cheek and moled on the chin. His bushy, brown hair tossed back from his forehead like a student's. His grey eyes flashed in kindly twinkles. His manners were engaging and winning, they said along Broadway, liking their little joke.

Refined art is never crude. 'Bud' Hauser did not go aboard ship with a dice cup in one pocket and a card pack in another and say, 'Come on, boys, try your luck.' Nothing like that. He had the professional man's calm. He was methodical. He approached the other man's money with no manifestation of enthusiastic zeal. He took it politely. A frank and unprejudiced person may approve of this method without endorsing the calling.

With Hauser it was a saying that the size of the gross determined the nerve for the net. Also, he was wont to repeat the adage, 'Actions speak louder than words,' the application of which will be understood by those who know commercial poker. No one ever thought of writing a play around deep-sea gambling until Hauser entered on his life work.

Capitalizing himself, for his large work was no small matter with this seagoing artist. In the blunt line of burglary, they will tell you what headquarters, a sweater and a cap and some jimmies of assorted sizes often answer. Check-raising requires primarily only a pen, but first cabin boob-catching is entirely different. It is the experience of the craftsman that there's almost as many halts and periods of chill in reaching out for a bankroll as there is in reaching out for the pole. So a campaign of preparation preceded every one of 'Bud' Hauser skirmishes with capital.

Fortunately for him, Hauser was made for evening clothes. He kept abreast of literature. He had dignified and sound opinions on European politics. He knew the views of Lombard Street on finance. He was forever meeting men on their own ground and thereby preparing them for the later coupon-cutting, at which he usually manages to be present.

All this took both time and money, but to 'Bud' Houser it was never irksome. He knew what he was after as well as he knew the three-mile limit offshore.

The name 'Bud' Houser never appeared on a passenger list. So long as he was present himself some other name always answered. He favored Berton Harvey for the most part on the Liverpool steamships and shaded off to something Frenchified if his destination was Cherbourg or Havre.

It was part of his art never to start a card game or propose a session with the dice. This is offered here as an example of his self-restraint. But he was ready with a yawn and what looked like an indifferent acceptance of an invitation to sit in. The pilot fish in petticoats sometimes called a bunco steerer, but he never complained of that. Once he was accused of petit larceny. That cut him to the quick, and forthwith he went to sea again.

But how is he died in harness, so to speak. He was homecoming on the *Olympic*, five days out from Southampton, or, as Hauser himself would have figured it, having in mind his smoking room activities, five nights out. He had been a busy man. The *Olympic* was like a mint. At early dogwatch on the morning of the fifth day Hauser cashed in his chips and went to his iced bath. He was not in the most perfect physical condition and the chill affected his heart.

A wireless message to shore mentioned the name of 'Bud' Hauser. The police did not answer this call. An undertaker did.

BIBLIOGRAPHY

LUODOVIC RADZEVIL

Nash, Jay R., *Hustlers and Con Men* (Evans & Co., 1976), pp.276–79.

'BUD' HAUSER

Charleston Gazette, 19 April 1912.
Denver Post, 16(?) April 1912.
New York American, 11 April 1912.
New York Evening Journal, 11 April 1912.
New York Herald, 11 and 18 April 1912.
New York Sun, 12 April 1912.
New York Tribune, 11 April 1912.
New York World, 10 and 11 April 1912.

GAMBLING TECHNIQUES AND DEVICES

Erdnase, S.W., *The Expert at the Card Table* (1902).
Gibson, Walter, *The Illustrated Book of Card Magic* (Doubleday, 1969).
Hayes, Sir Bertram, *Hull Down* (Macmillan Company, 1925).
Livingston, A.D., *Dealing With Cheats* (Lippincott, 1973).
MacDougall, Michael MacDonald, *Gamblers Don't Gamble* (1939).
Maskelyne, John Nevil, *Sharps and Flats* (Longman, Green & Co., 1894).

Quinn, John Phillip, *Gambling and Gambling Devices* (late 1800s).
Rostron, A.H., *Home from the Sea* (Macmillan, 1931).

GAMBLER ON THE *ADRIATIC*

Syracuse Herald, 27 February 1908.

HARRY SILBERBERG

Minneapolis Journal, 21 and 23 April 1912.
Minneapolis Tribune, 22 and 24 April 1912.
St. Paul Pioneer Press, 22 April 1912.

JAY YATES'S EARLY CAREER

Cleveland Plain Dealer, 21 April 1912.
Findlay Morning Republican, 22 and 24 April 1912.
Hancock Courier, 25 and 29 April 1912, 2 May 1912.
New York World, 21 April 1912.
Ohio State Journal, 21 April 1912.
Pittsburgh Post, 21 April 1912.
Washington Post, 21 April 1912.

Behe, George, 'Letter to "Sea Poste"', *The Commutator*, 26:159 (2002).
Brouwer, M., posting with genealogical information (groups.google.com/
    forum/#!msg/alt.genealogy/7PDxRJRfvRM/7tocKsd1VFIJ).
Fitch, Patrick, 'The Findlay Fugitive', *The Commutator*, 20:3 (November 1996–
    January 1997).
Fitch, Patrick, 'Jay Yates Returns', *The Commutator*, 23:148 (2000).
O'Hern, Dale, undated private communication with the author. Mr O'Hern,
    grandson of Hanna Yate's sister, writes: 'I at one time had cards from him
    [Jay Yates] to my aunt [Hanna], mentioning that he would be sailing on the
    Titanic, but unfortunately they were destroyed when our home burned in
    1958. They were found in her [Hanna's] home when she died, and left it to
    my grandmother.'
Yates, Wallace, letters to author (28 September and 10 October 1981).

THE GAMBLERS 'ANTHONY MELODY' AND 'J.W. WHITE'

Baltimore American, 16 April 1912 [first-class passenger list].

Board of Trade Southampton Departure List.
Klistorner, Daniel, 'A Thorough Analysis of the Cave List', *Encyclopedia Titanica* (www.encyclopedia-titanica.org/the-cave-list.html).
Titanic first-class passenger list issued to passengers.

HARRY HOMER'S EARLY CAREER

Akron Daily Democrat, 8 April 1902.
Chicago Inter Ocean, 12 April 1900.
Denver Post, 8 May 1912.
Indianapolis News, 25 April 1912.
Indianapolis Star, 24 April 1912.
Louisville Courier-Journal, 25 April 1912.
Louisville Times, 25 April 1912.
Newport News Daily Press, 5 July 1906.
New York Sun, 1 January 1902.
South Bend Times, 19 April 1912 [list of survivors].
The Times-Democrat, 24 November 1908.
Toronto Star, 17 April 1912 [Cherbourg passenger list].

Herbold, Mike, 'The Cruises of Harry Homer', unpublished research report.
Lynch, Don, letter to author (19 November 1992) [*Olympic* passenger lists in THS collection].
Stringer, Craig, '*Titanic* People', CD-ROM [Homer's full name].
'US Album of Criminals', quoted on *Encyclopedia Titanica* (www.encyclopedia-titanica.org/titanic-survivor/harry-homer.html).

GEORGE BRERETON'S EARLY CAREER

London Globe and Traveler, 19 April 1912 [Bereton's cabin on the *Titanic*].

Gowan, Philip, personal research on George Brereton's life.
Herbold, Mike, 'The Cruises of Harry Homer', unpublished research report [Brereton's voyages].
Söldner, Hermann, email to author [Brereton's voyages].
Stringer, Craig, '*Titanic* People', CD-ROM.

CHARLES ROMAINE'S EARLY CAREER

Encyclopedia Titanica (www.encyclopedia-titanica.org/).
Harris, Phil (a Romaine relative), letters to the author.
Söldner, Hermann, email to author [Romaine's voyages].
Stringer, Craig, '*Titanic* People', CD-ROM.

PREPARATIONS FOR THE VOYAGE AND GAMBLERS SAID TO BE ON BOARD

Los Angeles Times, 20 April 1912.
New York Evening World, 19 April 1912.
New York Herald, 18 April 1912.
New York Times, 18 April 1912.
Philadelphia Evening Bulletin, 18 April 1912.

EVENTS ON BOARD THE *TITANIC* DURING THE MAIDEN VOYAGE

Barkworth, Algernon, *Bennington Evening Banner*; *New York Times*, 19 April 1912.
Behr, Karl, *Brooklyn Daily Eagle*, 19 April 1912; *New York Tribune*, 20 April 1912.
Bird, Ellen, *New York World*, 20 April 1912.
Blank, Henry, *Newark News*, 19 April 1912.
Brandeis, Emil, *Omaha World Herald*, 19 April 1912; *Omaha News*, 23 April 1912;
    Denver Post, 8 May 1912.
Bullock, Shan, *Thomas Andrews, Shipbuilder* (Maunsel & Company, Ltd, 1912).
Carter, William, *Philadelphia Inquirer*, 21 April 1912.
Clark, Virginia, *Los Angeles Times*, 25 April 1912; *Los Angeles Herald*, 25 April 1912;
    The Commutator, Spring 1979; *New York Times*, 20 April 1912.
Clark, Walter, information about Walter Clark's alcoholism and being intoxicated that
    night comes from Don Lynch, who learned it from Clark's son's first wife's brother.
Dodge, Washington, *Loss of the Titanic* (1912).
Douglas, Mahala, *Minneapolis Journal*, 20 April 1912.
Dowdell, Elizabeth, *The Jersey Journal*, 19 April 1912.
Futrelle, May, *New York Sun*, 19 April 1912; *Seattle Daily Times*, 21–22 April 1912.
Gracie, Archibald, Senate *Titanic* investigation, pp.990, 1004 (www.titanicinquiry.org).
Gracie, Archibald, 'The Truth about the *Titanic*' (1913) [Elizabeth Shutes's
    recollections].
Graham, Edith, *New York Evening World*, 19 April 1912; *New York Times*, 20 April 1912.
Harris, Renée, *Omaha World Herald*, 19 April 1912; *New York Evening World*, 19 April
    1912; *Liberty* magazine, 23 April 1932.

Kimball, Edwin, *Boston Globe*, 19 April 1912.

Mellinger, Madeleine, letter to Walter Lord, Lord-Macquitty collection, National Maritime Museum, courtesy of Paul Lee (www.paullee.com/titanic/Mellinger.php).

Nourney, Alfred, *Brooklyn Daily Eagle*, 23 April 1912; *New York Sun*, 24 April 1912.

Peuchen, Arthur, *New York Sun*, 20 April 1912; Senate *Titanic* investigation, p.332.

Ray, Fred, Senate *Titanic* investigation, p.801.

Seward, Fred, *Berkshire Evening Eagle* (Pittsfield, MA), 23 April 1912.

Silverthorne, Spencer, *Indianapolis News*, 19 April 1912. The source for Silverthorne knowing that professional gamblers were participating in the bridge game is Walter Lord's notes as presented on Charles Pellegrino's website (www.charlespellegrino.com/passengers/spencer_v_silverthorne.htm).

Smith, Eloise, *Huntington Herald Dispatch*, 19 April 1912; Senate *Titanic* investigation, p.1149.

Steffanson, Hokan Björnström, *New York Tribune*, 19 April 1912.

Thayer, Marian, *Philadelphia Inquirer*, 21 April 1912.

Woolner, Hugh, *New York Tribune*, 19 April 1912; *New York Sun*, 19 April 1912; Senate *Titanic* investigation, p.883.

GAMBLER ACTIVITIES IN THE LIFEBOAT

Logan, Thomas, *Philadelphia Inquirer*, 21 April 1912.

GAMBLERS AFTER BOARDING THE *CARPATHIA*

Futrelle, May, *Seattle Daily Times*, 21 and 22 April 1912.

Harris, Renée, *Liberty* magazine, 23 April 1932.

New York American, 18 April 1912 [gambler interview on board the *Carpathia*].

Silverthorne, Spencer, pre-1955 account about Charles Romaine sent to Walter Lord (www.charlespellegrino.com/passengers/spencer_v_silverthorne.htm).

GAMBLER MARCONIGRAMS FROM THE *CARPATHIA*

Bennington Evening Banner, 20 April 1912.

New Orleans Daily Picayune, 18 April 1912.

New York Herald, 18 April 1912.

Booth, John, *Titanic: Signals of Disaster* (1993) [Homer and Brereton Marconigrams].

FIRST GAMBLER INTERVIEWS
IN NEW YORK USING ALIASES

'Bradley, George', *New York Evening Herald*, 23 April 1912.
'Brayton, George', *Brooklyn Daily Eagle*, 19 April 1912.
'Haven, H.', *New York Tribune*, 19 April 1912; *New York American*, 19 April 1912.
'Rotheld, C.', *Boston Globe*, 19 April 1912.

GAMBLER INTERVIEWS
USING THEIR TRUE NAMES

Homer, Harry, *Denver Post*, 8 May 1912.
Romaine, C.H., *New York World*, 21 April 1912; *New York Evening Journal*, 19 April 1912.

GAMBLER GROUP INTERVIEWS AND
UNNAMED GAMBLER INTERVIEWS

Buffalo Morning Express, 24 April 1912.
New York American, 24 April 1912.
New York Sun, 28 April 1912.
New York World, 24 April 1912.
Omaha News, 23 April 1912.
Washington Times, 3 May 1912.

INFORMATION ABOUT HOMER'S AND
ROMAINE'S CLAIMS FOR DAMAGES

National Archives, Bayonne, New Jersey.

RUMOURS IN ENGLAND ABOUT THE GAMBLERS
(WOMEN'S CLOTHES, 'DOC' OWEN, ETC.)

London Daily Chronicle, 27 April 1912.
New York Sun, 28 April 1912.
Western Daily Mercury, 30 April 1912.

BIBLIOGRAPHY

JOHN BADENOCH'S ATTEMPT TO CONTACT THE GAMBLERS AFTER THE SINKING

Brooklyn Daily Eagle, 19 April 1912.
New York Herald, 19 April 1912.
New York World, 23 April 1912.

GEORGE BRERETON'S ATTEMPT TO SWINDLE *TITANIC* SURVIVOR CHARLES STENGEL

New York Sun, 26 and 28 June 1912.

DENVER – 'CAPITAL OF CON'

Nash, Jay R., *Hustlers and Con Men* (Evans & Co., 1976), pp.214–15.

MRS PATTERSON AND EMIL BRANDEIS

Denver Post, 26, 27, 30 April; 5, 6, 8 and 12 May 1912.
Omaha News, 23 April 1912.

JAY YATES'S LATER LIFE

Daily Reports from Baltimore, vol. 10, 1 September 1911 to 30 November 1912; *Daily Report of Agent, US Secret Service*, 10 June 1912, p.2.
Findlay Morning Republican, 22 and 24 April 1912.
Hancock Courier, 25, 29 April, 2 May and 13 June 1912.
Washington Times, 3 May 1912 [interview with unnamed gambler, probably Brereton].

Fitch, Patrick, 'The Findlay Fugitive', *The Commutator*, 20:3 (November 1996–January 1997).
Fitch, Patrick, 'Jay T. Yates Returns: Findlay Fugitive on the Run', *The Commutator*, 23:148 (2000).
Fitch, Patrick, 'Findlay Fugitive Finally Found', *The Commutator*, 26:157 (2002).
Mellinger, Madeleine, letter to Walter Lord, Lord-Macquitty collection, National Maritime Museum, courtesy of Paul Lee (www.paullee.com/titanic/Mellinger.php).
Molony, Senan, 'Legendary Onboard Gambler Revealed as Historic Hoax', *Voyage*, 94 (Winter 2015–16).
Silvey, Alice, *Duluth Herald*, 1 May 1912; *Duluth News Tribune*, 2 May 1912.
Yates, Wallace B., letters to author, 28 September and 10 October 1981.

HARRY HOMER'S LATER LIFE

Albany Evening Journal, 1915.
Chicago Tribune, 12 November 1915.
Hamilton Daily News, 8 March 1939 [obituary/estate news].
Los Angeles Herald, 30 September 1915.
San Francisco Examiner, 18 May 1926.
South Bend News Times, 30 September 1915.
Tulsa Daily World, 2, 29 and 30 March 1919.

Booth, John, '*Titanic*: Signals of Disaster' [Homer Marconigram to wife].
Ellis Island arrival records, courtesy of Don Lynch [Homer's voyages].
Ellis Island arrival records, courtesy of Hermann Söldner [Homer's voyages].
Gowan, Philip, personal research on Harry Homer.
Herbold, Mike, 'The Cruises of Harry Homer', unpublished research report.

CHARLES ROMAINE'S LATER LIFE

Anderson Herald, 21 and 22 January 1922 [obituary].
Anderson Herald Bulletin, 12 April 2002.
Knightstown Banner, 29 September 1939, courtesy of Don Lynch [article describing
    William Homer's visit to the city].
New York City Directory 1921/1922 [Romaine's street address].
New York Times, 14 May 1921 [bankruptcy].
New York Times, 19 January 1922 [obituary].

Eaton, Jack, letter to the author (20 October 1981) [Romaine's street address in 1912
    is not listed in the *New York City Directory*].
Ellis Island sailing records, courtesy of Hermann Söldner [Romaine's voyages].
Lynch, Don, letter to author.

GEORGE BRERETON'S LATER LIFE

Aberdeen Daily News, 4 December 1909, courtesy of Mike Herbold [early info about
    the Maybury Gang].
Cincinnati Enquirer, 30 January 1915.
Los Angeles Examiner, 22 and 25 February 1922; 17 July 1942.
Los Angeles Times, 5 July 1933; 17 July 1942.
New York Sun, 24 October 1915.
New York Tribune, 26 and 28 June 1912.
Oakland Tribune, 11 April 1939.

San Diego Union, 5 July 1933, courtesy of Mike Herbold.
San Marcos Times & Daily News Leader, 24 December 1937.
Washington Post, 11 April 1915.

Ellis Island arrival records, courtesy of Don Lynch [Brereton's voyages].
Ellis Island arrival records, courtesy of Hermann Söldner [Brereton's voyages].
'George Brayton' letter to Nelson White (12 May 1912), courtesy of Don Lynch.
Herbold, Mike, 'Presumed Guilty: The Sad Story of Grace A. Brereton', *The Commutator*, 40:209 (May–July 2015).

GAMBLER LEGENDS

MacDougall, Michael, *Gamblers Don't Gamble* (Greystone Press, 1939).
Nash, Jay R., *Hustlers and Con Men* (Evans & Co., 1976).

LIST OF ILLUSTRATIONS

INDEX

INDEX